Horse's Health
Problem Solver

Roberta Baxter MRCVS

David and Charles

For Potter and my other
four-limbed friends

Acknowledgements

Many thanks are due to the staff and clients of the Old Golfhouse Veterinary Practice Ltd, without whom this book would not have been possible.

Thanks also to Caroline and Jo Baxter, Roz Cole and Theo Gould for proofreading the manuscript, and to Adam and Eddie for letting me get on with it.

Picture acknowledgements

All photographs/illustrations **by the author** except the following:

Horsepix.co.uk: pp endpapers, opp title page, 36, 40, 80, 98, 122, 137
Maggie Raynor: pp 6(rt), 8
David & Charles/Bob Langrish: p7(top)
Kit Houghton: pp 7(btm rt), 10(top), 69
David & Charles/Horsepix: pp 17, 47, 55, 57(left), 58(btm left & rt), 70(top), 108, 110, opp152
Dr Derek Knottenbelt/Equine Dept, Faculty of Veterinary Science, The University of Liverpool: pp 18(btm), 96, 104, 130(left), 140
Mrs Theo Gould: pp 19, 32
Susan McBane: 25(btm)
Colin Vogel: pp 44(ragwort, yew) p65(top),68, 100
David & Charles/Karl Adamson: p44(redmaple)
David & Charles/Andrew Perkins: p57(top, ctre & btm rt), 58(top left)
Karen Coumbe: p106
Andrew Carter: p109
Tony & Marcy Pavord: pp131, 132(top)
David & Charles/Paul Bale: pp 144–7

X-ray images: Old Golfhouse Veterinary Group, Thetford, Norfolk

A DAVID & CHARLES BOOK

First published in the UK in 2005

Copyright © Roberta Baxter 2005

Distributed in North America
by F&W Publications, Inc.
4700 East Galbraith Road
Cincinnati, OH 45236
1-800-289-0963

Roberta Baxter has asserted her right to be identified as author of this work in accordance with the Copyright, Designs and Patents Act, 1988.

A catalogue record for this book is available from the British Library.

ISBN 0 7153 1801 2

Horse care and riding is not without risk, and while the author and publishers have made every attempt to offer accurate and reliable information to the best of their knowledge and belief, it is presented without any guarantee. The author and publishers therefore disclaim any liability incurred in connection with using the information contained in this book.

Printed in China by SNP Leefung
for David & Charles
Brunel House   Newton Abbot   Devon

Commissioning Editor: Jane Trollope
Art Editor: Sue Cleave
Desk Editor: Louise Crathorne
Project Editor: Anne Plume
Production: Beverley Richardson

Visit our website at www.davidandcharles.co.uk

David & Charles books are available from all good bookshops; alternatively you can contact our Orderline on (0)1626 334555 or write to us at FREEPOST EX2110, David & Charles Direct, Newton Abbot, TQ12 4ZZ (no stamp required UK mainland).

Contents

Introduction

The aim of this book is to provide both novice and experienced horse owners with an up-to-date, easily accessible reference that will help them to deal with any problems their horses might have. The book contains useful, current information on a variety of equine issues and a range of diseases. With chapters on basic health care, feeding, exercise, preventative medicine, first aid and common diseases, this problem-solving guide is a comprehensive text that should provide horse owners with the information they need to keep their horses on top form.

Throughout the book, details are explained clearly with the aid of information boxes, and references to a detailed glossary. Combined with cross-referencing of linked information, this helps the book to be accessible and easy to understand. There is practical advice explaining how to carry out a variety of procedures ranging from emergency removal of shoes to appropriate bandaging of injuries, with plenty of photographs and diagrams to help illustrate the details within the text, enabling owners to translate reference information into action.

I hope that this book will be equally useful to the novice horse owner and to the more knowledgeable professional, helping all their horses to lead happy, healthy lives.

4

Choosing a horse for health

Keeping your horse healthy and safe

Preventative health care

I'm buying a new horse: how can I choose a healthy one?

Choosing a new horse is always difficult, and with the extensive choice that's usually available it can be hard to know where to start.

The first thing to consider is exactly what is wanted: someone experienced might want a young horse to bring on, whilst a novice rider may be looking for a schoolmaster. Whatever the buyer's requirements, it is important to have them in mind at all times in order to avoid purchasing a horse that is unsuitable, or unable to cope with the demands that will be placed on it.

Secondly: know where to look. The pages of advertising papers contain some genuine horses, and many dealers rely on a good reputation to keep their business going, but many horses that are for sale have underlying problems. To avoid the pitfalls it is important to know what to look for and which questions to ask. It is a good idea to take along an experienced, objective person to take a good look at any potential purchase, and ideally, to see it being ridden.

Whilst few horses have perfect conformation, it is important to take time to look at the shape of a horse, since those that are better 'put together' will be less prone to injury than those that have certain conformational abnormalities.

Having seen the horse at rest, it is also a good idea to see it trotted in hand on a firm surface. At this time one can look for signs of lameness (Lameness p119) as well as making a note of the arc that each limb takes as it travels through the air – again, asymmetries that involve plaiting, brushing or dishing of limbs can be associated with an increased susceptibility to injury. When trying the horse out, it is a good idea to have an experienced person with you, who can also watch for signs of lameness. Make sure that all his paces are tried on a variety of surfaces, and work on both reins; this should reveal any subtle lameness that only tends to show up at exercise on a particular rein (usually the rein that has the affected limb on the inside of the circle).

Finally, if the horse seems ideal, ask the vendor

know-how: Basic points of conformation

When looking at a horse for the first time, it should be stood up square on a firm surface, to enable an objective assessment of its conformation.

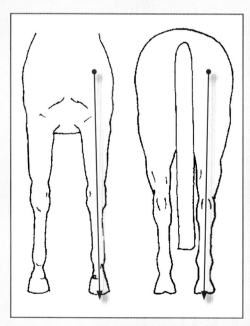

- The legs should be straight when they are viewed from in front or behind, and the joints should be positioned in line one above the other; they should not be offset (*left*). A horse which has poor limb conformation will have asymmetric stresses passing through its joints as it moves, and this will in turn predispose to wear and tear on the affected joints and can lead to early arthritic changes.

- The feet should be symmetrical, and the shape of the hooves should match so they make a pair at the front and a pair at the back. Many low-grade lamenesses will cause changes in the shape of the affected foot: it will usually become more upright and 'boxy' with reduced use.

From the side, the front and rear walls of the hoof should be parallel, and the mid-point of the coffin joint (which lies one-third of the way back along the coronary band) should lie directly above the middle of the weight-bearing surface of the foot or shoe (*below*).

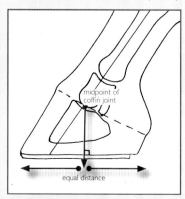

midpoint of coffin joint

equal distance

about its likes and dislikes. It is a good idea to find out whether it can tolerate a straw bed in its stable and hay to eat, or whether it is sensitive to dust and needs dust-free management (Respiratory disease p96). Enquiries should be made concerning vices (Vices p50) such as crib-biting, windsucking and weaving, as all can predispose to medical problems. A guarantee regarding absence of vices can always be requested, and horses showing vices within a period of, say, one week, may be returned to the vendor if the vendor agrees this in writing.

It is also worth enquiring whether the vendor will allow the horse to be loaned for a limited 'trial' period; this will give you the chance to see how well the horse meets your requirements. However, many vendors are understandably cautious about allowing a horse into someone else's care, as accidents do happen. From this point of view it is a good idea to ensure that any loaned horses are fully insured.

Having a healthy horse encompasses having a fit horse without underlying physical or psychological problems, that is suited to the job it is intended for. Finding such a horse is no easy feat, and takes time and patience!

■ A pre-purchase examination should include examination at exercise.

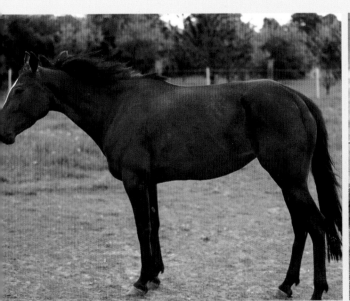

■ Other aspects of conformation that are important include the set of the limbs and their contour, the strength of the limbs (often referred to in terms of inches of bone), the breadth of the chest, and the set of the head on the neck. In addition, it is important to look at the shape of the back – obviously a 'roach' (*left*) or 'sway' (*right*) back can be associated with back problems and is not ideal.

What type of pre-purchase veterinary examination should I have?

Once a suitable horse has been found, the next step should be to arrange for it to be checked over by a vet before any money changes hands. This allows any underlying medical problems (there are few perfect horses!) to be identified, and gives you the chance to assess whether or not these are likely to prevent the horse from doing the job it is intended for.

Several types of veterinary pre-purchase examination are available, the exact format of which varies between countries. In the UK the five-stage vetting, which is equivalent to the full examination that most insurance companies will request at the inception of a policy, is the gold-standard test for the equine pre-purchase examination. This examination follows a particular structure adopted by vets across the country, and encompasses a thorough clinical examination (Stage 1), examination at in-hand exercise (Stage 2), examination during more strenuous exercise (Stage 3), examination during rest after exercise (Stage 4), and a final exercise period after rest (Stage 5). In the USA the exact format of equine pre-purchase examinations is less rigorously prescribed; however, a thorough examination should include assessment of the same factors.

know-how: Ageing horses

It is important to be aware that ageing a horse by its teeth gives only an indication of likely age and can be extremely inaccurate. However, some knowledge of the changes that occur to most horses' teeth with time can allow owners to guesstimate a horse's age; this is most accurate when applied to young horses.

The most useful factors to be aware of are the eruption times of the incisor teeth, and the changes in wear and appearance of these teeth. Horses with dental disease or abnormal wear – for instance, due to crib-biting; see Vices p50 – are subject to greater inaccuracies in age estimation.

ERUPTION TIMES
The deciduous ('milk') incisors have a whiter and more fragile appearance, with a more rounded edge at the gum line, than the permanent incisors. The eruption times from central (the middle of the

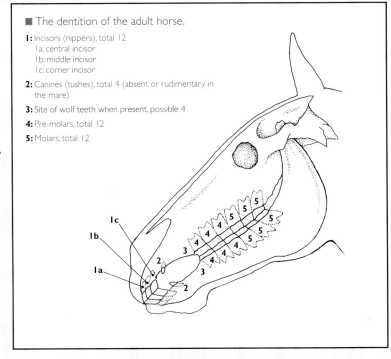

■ The dentition of the adult horse.

1: Incisors (nippers), total 12
   1a: central incisor
   1b: middle incisor
   1c: corner incisor

2: Canines (tushes), total 4 (absent or rudimentary in the mare)

3: Site of wolf teeth when present, possible 4

4: Pre-molars, total 12

5: Molars, total 12

A pre-purchase examination should include examination at exercise.

■ This four-year-old horse has his central and middle permanent incisors but has not yet replaced his corner deciduous incisors with permanent teeth. The ageing of such a horse could be reasonably accurate.

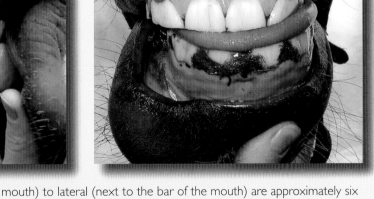

mouth) to lateral (next to the bar of the mouth) are approximately six days, six weeks and six months for the deciduous teeth, and 2.5, 3.5 and 4.5 years for the permanent incisors. The permanent teeth usually come into wear with their opposing teeth around nine months after eruption, so that a horse with a 'full mouth' in wear is usually more than five years old. In a young horse the incisor teeth tables (the wearing surfaces) are usually oval, but with age they become more triangular.

(continued over)

In some cases a 'limited' pre-purchase examination is used, which incorporates Stages 1 and 2 of the full examination. This is a less strenuous examination that is performed when examining unbroken horses for purchase, and is equivalent to the 'mortality' examination sometimes required by insurance companies. Whilst it can allow the identification of a number of problems, many diseases, including low-grade lamenesses, won't necessarily show up, so a more thorough examination is usually advisable for working horses.

In either case it is important to use an experienced horse vet, not only to help recognize and identify any problems that are present, but also to assess whether any abnormalities that are discovered will or will not, 'on the balance of probabilities', prevent the horse from doing the job that it is being purchased for.

A full five-stage pre-purchase

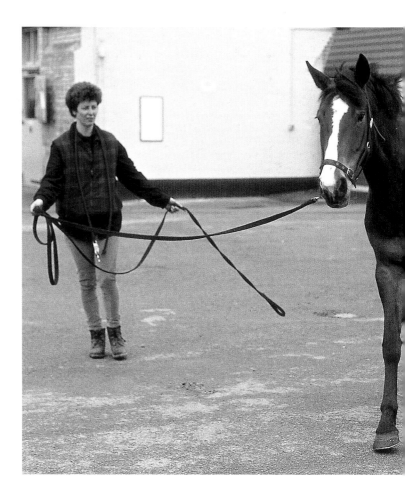

know-how: *Ageing horses*

New incisor teeth have a hollow in the table, called the infundibulum, which wears out with age, usually disappearing by approximately six, eight and ten years of age (from central to lateral); a mark can remain in the area until the early to mid-teens. At the same time (around six, eight and ten years) a new mark called the dental star appears between the infundibulum and the inner surface of the teeth.

Other characteristics that can be helpful, but which are less predictable, include the development of a 'hook' on the edge of each upper corner incisor adjacent to the bar of the mouth at around seven and 13 years, and the presence of a mark (Galvayne's groove) that appears on the outer surface of the corner incisors and moves from the gum towards the wearing surface of the teeth between around 10 and 20 years of age.

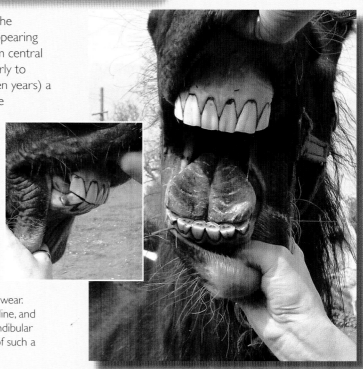

■ This 12-year-old horse has all her permanent incisors in wear. Galvayne's groove is restricted to the area of the gum line, and the tables of the teeth are triangular with both an infundibular mark and dental star present. An approximate ageing of such a horse could be possible.

examination should normally start in the stable, with the horse having been kept in for a couple of hours prior to examination so that any stiffness or dust-associated breathing disease has a chance to show up. A full clinical examination, including a thorough check of the eyes, ears, nose, teeth (which allows approximate ageing: see Ageing p8), skin, heart, lungs and musculo-skeletal system, is carried out.

After this, the horse may be trotted up on a firm surface in hand and lunged, before proceeding to a period of ridden exercise (for riding horses) or other strenuous exercise at walk, trot, canter and gallop on both reins. This allows evaluation of stride and lameness, breathing noise and heart performance. Afterwards it is a good idea to rest the horse for a brief period before trotting him up again, because at this stage some lamenesses show up that are only

■ Lungeing on a firm surface to check for lameness

evident after rest that follows exercise. Flexion tests that can unmask lameness (Flexion tests p120) may also be carried out, and some nerve function tests (Neurological tests p140) are employed.

Further tests that can be done include survey radiographs (Radiography p121) of the joints to evaluate whether degenerative joint disease (DJD) (Arthritis p135) and other joint problems are present; endoscopy (Endoscopy p96) if respiratory disease is suspected; and then finally ultrasonography (Ultrasonography p112) if any potential tendon or ligament lesions are found. Other tests may also be recommended in certain cases. In addition, blood can be taken and either submitted for secure storage for up to six months, or tested for the presence of pain-relieving medicines and sedatives, giving both vendors and buyers some protection should the horse have a problem after purchase.

■ This 25-year-old horse has all his permanent incisors in wear, and they are long and worn. Galvayne's groove is extensive (but hard to see clearly, due to tooth discoloration). Accurate ageing by dentition would be impossible, though such a horse could be said to be 'aged'.

Should I insure my horse? What types of insurance are advisable?

Not only is insurance extremely useful when those unexpected vets' bills crop up – and with the cost of a surgical colic running into thousands of pounds, insurance is a must if you want to keep your horse's treatment options open – but it is also important for a number of other reasons. Probably the most important of these is public liability insurance: don't forget that owners are responsible for their horses and also for any damage they might cause, and may be held so legally. Most of the cheaper horse insurance policies also include personal accident, the value of the horse at death, and its value in the event of either theft or of straying.

The next level of policies should include cover for vets' fees, tack, stables and the temporary hire of a replacement horse if one is stolen. However, many illnesses prevent a horse from being able to work but without necessitating its euthanasia, under which circumstances normal insurance will not pay out the horse's value. A further option, which is extremely useful in such cases, is loss of use insurance. This pays out the pre-injury value of a horse if it develops a condition that does not necessitate euthanasia but does render it unable to fulfil its original function; this means that the owner can afford to purchase a new mount.

It can be depressing to have to make treatment choices for a sick animal that are based on finances rather than what is actually best for the horse, so it is usually advisable to insure horses against vets' fees as well as the basic public liability insurance. Another option that some owners choose is to put a certain amount of money aside each month for emergencies, and this can work quite well. The main thing is to avoid having an empty bank account just when your horse decides to injure itself.

■ Whatever the function of your horse or pony, insurance is advisable.

Does my insurance cover me if my horse sees other practitioners?

Insurance for vets' fees pays for the fees of the horse's first opinion vet. If a second opinion or a referral to a hospital facility is sought, then the insurance company must be informed prior to the referral/second opinion appointment, and they will decide whether or not to authorize further costs, or will set a limit on such costs. In practice, insurance companies rarely have any problem with referral of horses for further investigation and treatment at an equine hospital (given that the total cost falls within that allowed by the policy), but they may not authorize payment for a second opinion if they do not consider such an appointment to be necessary.

Where complementary or alternative medicine practitioners are concerned, their assistance with a case must be recommended by the vet, and before such treatment is initiated, advice should be sought from the insurance company as to whether or not they will cover such costs. Again, in practice, most insurance companies cover treatments that are recommended by the vet such as physiotherapy, acupuncture and chiropractic treatment, as long as they are carried out by reputable practitioners who have completed the necessary training. Such

practitioners should always check with a horse's vet before assessing or treating the horse, in order to ensure that such treatments are appropriate in each particular case.

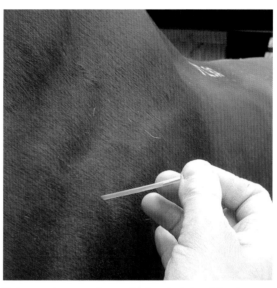

■ Acupuncture needles can be inserted at points where they have an effect on the nervous system.

know-how: Complementary therapies

What is physiotherapy?
Physiotherapy is a non-invasive therapy that involves working on a horse's muscles and other soft tissues to improve mobility and reduce pain. It can be useful in horses that have had limb or back injuries, and it may improve their quality of life and performance. Licensed physiotherapists (Contacts p150) should only ever be used, and only on the advice of a veterinary surgeon.

What is acupuncture?
Acupuncture involves putting fine needles through the skin and into the underlying tissues in locations where they can have an effect on the nervous system. It can be used for treating a wide range of conditions but is most often used to treat back and limb pain and stiffness. Acupuncture treatment of horses should only be carried out by veterinary acupuncturists (Contacts p150).

What is chiropractic treatment?
Chiropractic treatment involves working on the soft tissues and bones of a horse to improve mobility and reduce pain. Like physiotherapy, it is often used to treat head, back or limb pain or stiffness, and should only be carried out by licensed practitioners on the recommendation of a vet (Contacts p150).

What is homoeopathy?
Homoeopathy involves the use of various products at high dilution to treat a wide range of conditions with few side effects. Treatment of horses should only be carried out by vets registered to practise homoeopathy (Contacts p150).

What about herbs?
A number of herbs are available to treat a wide range of conditions in horses. They should only really be used on the advice of a veterinary surgeon.

How can I protect my horse against theft?

The first step for protecting horses against theft is good security. Stable yards and fields can be padlocked (don't padlock stables in case of fire), and it is important to chain and padlock the hinge side of a gate as well as the side that normally opens, so as to prevent thieves lifting it off its hinges.

Horses are safest at home or at a yard where someone is always on site. 'Horsewatch' and other neighbourly schemes help to protect horses against theft, and it is always a good idea to keep an eye out for any suspicious people or lorries, and to adopt the habit of recording the registration plate numbers of any unusual vehicles seen hanging around.

In the case of particularly valuable horses it may be helpful to avoid anything that identifies them individually to a stranger – for instance, personalized headcollars – although forms of individual identification, such as microchipping or freezebranding,

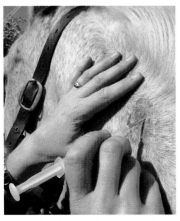

■ A microchip can be inserted for tamperproof identification.

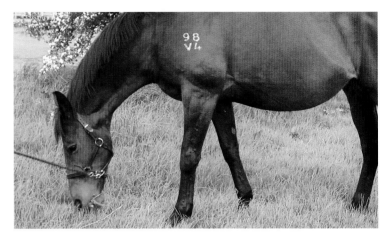

■ Freezemarking is a deterrent to potential thieves.

that will prove a horse or pony's ownership do deter thieves.

Microchips are probably the best form of identification as they are tamperproof (unless surgically removed). A microchip carries an individual number and is usually implanted into the ligament at the base of the mane on the left side of the neck using a wide bore needle. The procedure is slightly uncomfortable but does not normally require sedation or any more than the usual level of restraint. The number on the microchip is then logged with the owner's contact details on a national database. Stolen or stray horses can then be reunited with their owners after a chip scanner has been used to identify their individual chip. It is likely that microchipping will eventually become mandatory in order to enable individual identification of horses and their passports.

Despite the potential for

tampering with a brand, freeze-marking is useful because it is so immediately obvious to a potential thief. It marks the horse in the same way as a hot brand, but is much less painful and therefore easier. Lip tattooing can also be used to identify horses, but again the potential is there for tattoos to be tampered with, and both freezemarking and tattooing can also be difficult to read in some horses (particularly freezemarks in grey horses) as they don't always show up clearly. Finally, hoof branding can be used for identification, though obviously must be repeated every few months as the hoof grows out.

Other methods of identification that will enable a person to prove ownership include having an identification certificate completed by a vet, and keeping a set of photos taken from all angles. DNA testing can also be employed, and the results held with a horse's registration with a breed society or other equine organization.

How often should I get my horse's teeth checked?

Horses' teeth grow constantly throughout their life, wearing down as they grind their food. Horses therefore need regular dental treatment to correct any abnormalities of wear that arise from their teeth not meeting perfectly, or from their pattern of chewing being asymmetric. Even horses with teeth that meet well tend to develop sharp points on the outsides of the upper molars and the insides of the lower molars, which can cause cheek and tongue lacerations. At a regular dental check, a horse's teeth can be examined, any sharp points rasped smooth to prevent injury, and irregularities of wear treated by rasping, or electric burring in the case of problematic teeth. In addition, any teeth that are causing obvious problems with performance can be treated: wolf teeth can be removed, and the front molars can be 'bit-seated', which may help the horse in his response to the bit.

For many horses it is sufficient to check and treat the teeth once yearly, and this can be done by the vet at the time of the horse's annual vaccination and checkover. However, most horses over the age of 10, and some others that have abnormalities of wear, need their teeth checked and treated every six months, and in some cases even more often.

Should I use the dentist or a vet?

Most equine vets offer a dental service, so many horse owners prefer to use their vets for dental

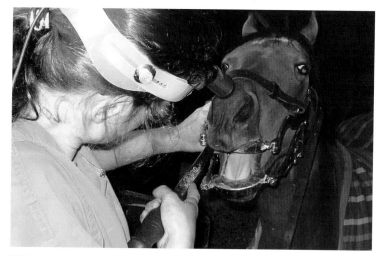

■ Using a gag or mouth speculum and a light, the teeth can be thoroughly examined and treated by a vet or equine dentist.

work. However, equine dental technicians are also available, and those that are well qualified have recently formed a professional body. Licensed equine dental technicians have completed a specified training and attained a certain level of practice, and have the necessary instrumentation to perform their job properly. By law they are allowed to carry out examinations and to treat dental overgrowths and sharp dental points. However, where intensive treatment is needed, a vet may also need to be present in order to sedate the horse prior to treatment, and to supervise any extractions.

Although many unqualified horse dentists do still practise, it is hard to know what their level of knowledge, training and of experience is; they are not covered by the relevant professional indemnity should a problem occur. Ideally, therefore,

horse owners should only use either vets or licensed equine dental technicians for their horses' dental care.

How to choose an equine dentist

As the equine dental profession is still in the process of inception, it can be hard to find out which practitioners in an area are properly trained and qualified to treat horses. However, local vets should be well placed to advise whom to use. Alternatively, more information about licensed equine dental technicians can be obtained from the British Equine Veterinary Association or the American Association of Equine Practitioners (Contacts p150) as well as the British Association of Equine Dental Technicians, and the World Wide Association of Equine Dentists (Contacts p150).

How often should I get the farrier out and where do I find one?

Most horses with good foot conformation and normal hoof growth that are shod and in work need to see the farrier every six weeks or so in order to maintain ideal foot balance. However, horses with abnormal hoof growth or that have problems requiring surgical farriery – laminitis, navicular syndrome, or cracks: see Lameness p119 – may need to be re-shod sooner, sometimes as often as every three to four weeks. On the other hand, those horses whose feet maintain a good shape and only grow slowly may need the farrier's attention much less frequently. In addition, some horses that are not shod (and with the recent trend for barefoot horses this is becoming more common) and that keep a good hoof shape as their feet wear down, may also require less frequent trimming.

As well as regular care from the farrier at whatever interval he or she recommends for each horse, it is also important to care for horses' feet by picking them out and removing stones and mud at least twice daily. Any solar injuries should be referred promptly to a vet as damage to the structures of the foot (Lameness p119) and sub-solar infections (Lameness p119) can occur. Some horses with poor hoof horn quality also benefit from food supplements that stimulate the growth of healthy and strong hoof horn and may reduce cracking, flaking and loss of shoes.

How do I choose a reliable farrier?

Finding a good farrier can be difficult, but local vets and other horse owners should be well placed to advise owners as to whom to use. Further information can be derived from the Farriers Registration Council (UK) or the American Farriers Association (Contacts p150), who keep a list of the qualified farriers in each area.

■ Regular farriery ensures foot balance is maintained, helping to prevent foot problems and lameness.

I'm confused about worming. What should I use, when and why?

Without an effective worming regime, horses are more likely to suffer from colic (Colic p102), weight loss (Weight loss p107) and diarrhoea (Diarrhoea p105). Haemorrhage and damage to the blood supply of the intestines can also occur, and some of these conditions can be fatal. Regular appropriate worming is of paramount importance in helping horses to stay healthy. Other measures to reduce horses' access to worms include regularly collecting faeces from the pasture; feeding hay in the field from racks, rather than the ground to avoid contamination; and not overcrowding pastures. Regular resting and reseeding of meadows can also be helpful, and rotating fields between different species can cut down on infective levels of larvae on the pasture.

There are many different ways to worm horses effectively, and the plethora of products on the market and advice available can make planning a worming regime extremely confusing. Some owners have regular faecal tests done and only worm when evidence of worm eggs or larvae is found in their

■ Regular collection of faeces from pastureland will help to keep the worm count down.

know-how: A worming plan

This plan can be adapted according to the particular needs of horses, depending on their management and environment on the advice of a local vet.

SPRING
Northern USA and UK:
Double dose tetrahydropyrimidine (eg Strongid P).
Southern USA:
Double dose tetrahydropyrimidine (eg Strongid P).

SUMMER
Northern USA and UK:
Regular doses of benzimidazoles (eg Panacur), tetrahydropyrimidines (eg Strongid P), or macrocyclic lactones (eg Eqvalan/ Equest/ Quest).
Southern USA:
Assess the need for worming, based on the weather.

AUTUMN
Northern USA and UK:
Double dose tetrahydropyrimidine (eg Strongid P).

Southern USA:
Double dose tetrahydropyrimidine (eg Strongid P) and regular doses of benzimidazoles (eg Panacur), tetrahydropyrimidines (eg Strongid P), or macrocyclic lactones (eg Eqvalan/ Equest/ Quest).

WINTER
Northern USA and UK:
Macrocyclic lactone with efficacy against encysted redworms as well as bots (eg Equest/ Quest).
Southern USA:
Macrocyclic lactone with efficacy against encysted redworms as well as bots (eg Equest/ Quest), and then assess the need for further worming, based on the weather.

■ Wormers can be given in feed, or straight into the mouth by syringe.

horses' dung; however, worms can be present and causing gut damage even when they are not passing detectable eggs in the horse's faeces. Others use a worming plan (Worming plan p17) that involves worming all the horses on a premises against the same types of worm with the same product at the time of year when that type of worm is most susceptible. This system can work well, as long as the worms on a particular premises are not resistant to the wormer that is being used; occasional pre- and post-worming faecal worm egg counts can be employed in order to check the efficacy of wormers. Finally, daily in-feed deworming is available in the USA and can be used with some success.

Whichever system is in use, any new horse on to a premises should be isolated, wormed with a broad spectrum wormer, and kept in for 24–48 hours to avoid seeding the pasture with large numbers of worm eggs. Thereafter all horses on the same premises should be wormed together with the same product for the best results (though this can be difficult in multi-owner livery yards).

For horses kept in the UK and the northern USA, a strategic worming plan should incorporate worming in December/January with a wormer containing a macrocyclic lactone (such as moxidectin) to kill bots and also encysted larval redworms (a five-day course of Panacur Guard can also be used to treat the latter). In March and September a double dose of a tetrahydropyrimidine wormer (for example, Strongid P) should be used to kill tapeworms.

Then from May to September wormers should be used at the intervals recommended by the manufacturers for the treatment of roundworms/redworms picked up from the pasture. To reduce the potential for the worms on a premises developing resistance to a wormer type, the wormers used can be rotated on a three-year cycle between a benzimidazole, a tetrahydropyrimidine and a macrocyclic lactone; however, since resistance to both of the former groups of wormers can occur, some yards use only the latter group.

In the southern USA, the different weather patterns mean that during the summer, worm eggs and larvae on the pastures are usually killed by the heat, whilst the pastures remain infective for roundworms and redworms well into the winter (when the cold in the north results in the worms hibernating). This means that the above programme needs to be adapted to ensure regular deworming through autumn and winter in the southern states, but that worming in the summer months is less important in this particular region.

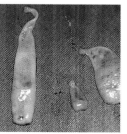

■ The most commonly encountered worms: redworms (*left*), roundworms (*centre*) and tapeworms (*right*)

What vaccinations are available? Which ones will my horse need?

The vaccinations most commonly used for horses are those that protect them against flu and tetanus, and competing horses must be fully vaccinated against these two diseases in order for them to be allowed to go to competitions. Flu is a highly infectious respiratory condition (Respiratory disease p96) that makes horses feel unwell and unable to work, and any horses that come into contact with others in large yards or out on hacks or at shows, or that have other horses nearby, will benefit from protection against flu. Tetanus bacteria (Tetanus p85) are found widely in the soil, and tetanus can easily result from contamination of a minor cut or graze, with potentially fatal results. Horses are particularly susceptible to this infection so, ideally, all horses should be protected against tetanus.

Other vaccines that are used widely include those for herpes virus. This condition causes rhinopneumonitis that is characterized by a highly infectious cough, together with an increased temperature and significant malaise (Respiratory disease p96); it can also cause neurological disease such as collapse, and it can cause abortion. For this reason many performance horses and most breeding mares are vaccinated against this disease.

In the USA, vaccines are also widely used against rabies (Neurological disease p140) and encephalomyelitis (Neurological disease p140), and vaccines against strangles (Respiratory disease p96), botulism, equine viral arteritis (Reproductive disease p114), Potomac horse fever, anthrax, equine protozoal myeloencephalitis (p140), rotavirus (gastro-intestinal disease p104) and salmonellosis (gastro-intestinal disease p104) are also available and can be used for at-risk horses.

■ Without regular vaccinations, horses are susceptible to a range of diseases and may not be allowed to compete.

How often do horses need vaccinating? How do I time it right?

For the combined flu and tetanus vaccinations, the initial course consists of two injections approximately one month apart, followed by a third injection after approximately six months, and then a yearly booster to maintain immunity. Competition horses may require six-monthly rather than yearly boosters.

The herpes virus vaccination protocol similarly necessitates two initial injections approximately one month apart, and then a booster every six months to maintain immunity.

Vaccinations should be given by veterinary surgeons only, and full details are entered on the horse's passport. For those horses that are competing, the injection intervals for flu and tetanus vaccination have to fall within the following time limits, otherwise horses must begin the process again and may not compete until at least the first two injections have been given. In order to comply with the Jockey Club requirements, the first two injections must be given with an interval of between 21–92 days between them, the third one 150–215 days after the second, and thereafter the current situation is that boosters must be given at intervals of no more than one calendar year, although this may be reduced to six months. The FEI guidelines differ slightly from this, in that after the two initial vaccinations given 21--92 days apart, boosters must be given within six months.

Where foals of less than four months are to take part in competitions, they are normally exempt from these requirements, provided that their dam's vaccines comply with the rules. Pregnant mares should, in any case, have had a flu and tetanus booster approximately four to six weeks before foaling in order to ensure that adequate immunity is passed to the young foal.

Herpes virus vaccines can also be given in pregnancy to reduce the risk of abortion.

How often do horses need checking over by a vet?

Where fit, healthy adult horses are concerned, a yearly check-over and frank discussion of any concerns felt at the time of vaccination is usually sufficient to ensure that no underlying problems are developing. However, horses on medication usually need to be checked over every three to six months to ensure that no side effects or new symptoms are occurring, and any horses that show signs of pain, distress or illness should obviously be seen promptly by their vet.

■ Any problems should be checked promptly by a vet.

What insects do I need to watch out for? How can I prevent problems?

A number of flies can cause problems in horses: these range from uncomfortable and infected bites, to distressed behaviour and headshaking (Headshaking p92), which in particular can seriously affect performance. In addition, blowflies will lay eggs in open wounds, and the maggots that hatch can then cause further damage (Fly strike p86). Flies may also have a role to play in the transmission of sarcoids (Sarcoids p82), and they can also pass on the papilloma virus that causes warts. Culicoides midges are also problematic: they can cause severe skin irritation, particularly in those horses that have an allergy to their saliva, which can develop 'sweet itch' (Sweet itch p84), and mosquitoes can also cause nasty bites.

Ticks are a problem in some parts of the country, usually being transmitted on to the pasture by sheep or deer. They attach to the limbs of horses to suck blood, and can transmit infections; these include Lyme's disease, which causes lethargy and arthritis (Arthritis p135).

Other insects that can cause disease include lice and mange (Skin disease p83), both of which are normally only transmitted directly from infested horses. It is therefore a good idea to isolate new arrivals, check them over carefully before they come into contact with other horses, and to put a double fence between different groups of horses to prevent contact over the fence. Any signs of skin disease should be investigated promptly by a vet.

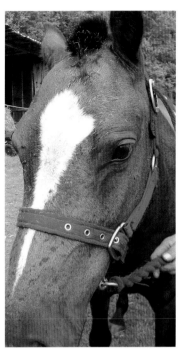

■ Flies can cause severe skin irritation.

know-how: *Preventing fly-related problems*

The problems caused by flies, midges, mosquitoes and ticks can all be prevented by being vigilant and dealing promptly with the situation with a number of measures.

■ **Insect repellents:**
There are a variety of products on the market, the most effective of which are available from vets.

Herbal fly repellents, particularly those containing citronella, can also be helpful, but may be less effective than those containing permethrin-based products.

'Frontline', a dog and cat flea product, is unlicensed for use in horses at this time, but is used successfully by many owners to prevent ticks and other parasites from causing problems, and some horse owners use cattle fly tags (also currently unlicensed in horses). These can be attached to the headcollar or mane, with good results.

■ **Fly masks** (*right*) **and fringes.**
■ **Fly strips and fly traps** can be used in stables but positioned well out of reach of the horse.

■ **'Sweet-itch' rugs** (that protect most of the body and neck) can be very useful.
■ **Keep horses away from open water in the summertime.**
■ **Pasture horses away from other species** (particularly cows, sheep and deer, which attract flies and pass on ticks).
■ **Remove muck promptly from areas near stables.**
■ **Stable horses at dawn and dusk.** This is when most of the flies and midges are about. Try turning them out at night rather than during the daytime in the summer months.

What tack and rugs do I need and how can I make sure they fit properly?

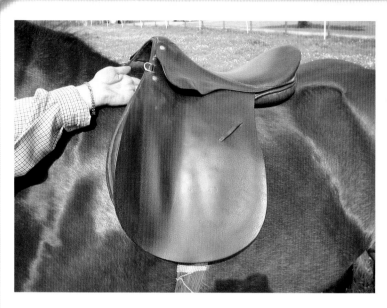

■ Saddles should be fitted by a saddler and checked regularly.

■ Bridles should be properly adjusted so that where snaffle bits are used, they make just one wrinkle at the corner of the mouth.

■ Poor saddle fit can result in back pain and the development of white marks on the withers.

The best person to advise on appropriate tack is a saddler – exactly what each horse needs depends on the job it does, and the riders it carries, as well as its own shape and size. It is also extremely important to make sure bridles are adjusted properly and that bits are appropriate and fit exactly. Saddles should be fitted and flocked (stuffed) to suit the individual horse's back, and re-flocked regularly as the shape of the horse changes due to weight loss, weight gain, or changes in muscling. Otherwise, ill-fitting tack commonly causes mouth injuries, back problems (Back pain p138), and very often bad behaviour and poor performance. For more information, contact the Society of Master Saddlers (UK) Ltd or the Master Saddlers Association (USA) (Contacts p150).

Saddlers and tack salespersons can also give advice about rugging. What each horse needs depends on its breed and type, the work it does, and whether or not it is clipped in winter. The minimum most horses need is some kind of turnout rug for winter, a sweat rug for drying off, and possibly a light fly rug for summertime. It is important to ensure that rugs fit properly so they don't rub.

Feeding principles

Feeding practice

Exercise

How do I know my horse is too fat or underweight?

Although there are exceptions, most horses that are the correct weight should have:

- ribs that can be felt, but not seen;
- a neck that is firm but not crested;
- a spine that is well covered, but doesn't have a crease or gutter along it;
- a back that is rounded, but not so fat that the bones of the pelvis can't be felt.

Horses that are overweight (see Feeding for weight reduction page 33) or underweight (see Feeding for weight gain page 35) are more prone to disease. Once the right weight for an individual horse has been established (and this will depend on its breed, type, function and health status), it is a good idea to monitor and record weight regularly – say, every three to four months – to ensure that it doesn't change.

■ Condition score 3: Cob. A reasonably fit cob that has substance but is not carrying too much weight.

know-how: Using a weight tape

1: Using a weight tape or tape measure, measure the horse or pony around its girth in centimetres (see photograph, right).

2: A weight tape gives an immediate conversion to approximate weight in kilogrammes. If using a tape measure, the following formula gives the same information:

Weight (kg) = $\dfrac{\text{Girth}^2 \text{ (cm)} \times \text{Length from point of shoulder* to point of hip* (cm)}}{11,877}$

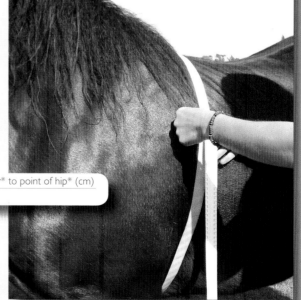

*see Anatomy page 144

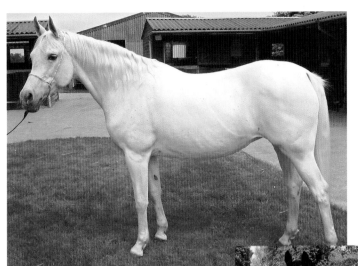

Condition scoring can help the horse owner to remain objective, as can regular weight taping (see opposite). Generally we should aim for all horses to have a condition score of 3; however, exceptions to this include ponies that are prone to laminitis (see Laminitis page 122), whose condition score should ideally be aimed at 2–2.5 to help avoid this condition. Many show horses and ponies are kept at a condition score nearer 4, although this is not always ideal.

■ Condition score 3: Arab. A much lighter build than the cob, and less prone to obesity, this is a good weight for an Arab.

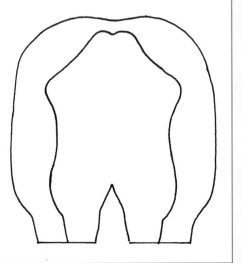

■ Condition score 3: Thoroughbred. Different breeds need to be assessed according to their type, but the same weight checks apply.

know-how: How to condition score a horse

Look at the horse from behind, and score the pelvis, then check the neck and back and adjust the score up or down by one grade if necessary.

■ When viewed from the rear, the outer line represents 5 on the condition scale and the inner line 0. Ideal condition will fall about halfway between the two.

0: Thin: angular pelvis; sunken rump with cavity under tail; prominent ribs and spine; and marked 'ewe' neck.

1: Poor: prominent pelvis, cavity under tail, obvious ribs and spine, and a narrow neck.

2: Moderate: rump flat on either side of spine; ribs and spine just apparent; and neck narrow but firm.

3: Good: rump rounded; pelvis easily palpable; ribs and spine covered, but palpable, firm neck.

4: Fat: rump fleshy, with gutter in the midline; pelvis, ribs and spine hard to feel; neck is wide with a slight crest.

5: Obese: the rump is fat with a deep gutter in the midline; the pelvis, ribs and spine cannot be felt; there is a gutter along the back, the neck is wide and crested.

Can you give me some basic advice as to what nutrients horses need?

Like us, horses have basic requirements for water, energy, protein and certain essential vitamins and minerals (principally vitamins A, B and E; and calcium, phosphorus, magnesium, sodium, chloride and potassium). Some horses can derive all their requirements from the forage (that is grass, hay, haylage or silage) in their diet. In the summer, good quality grass may meet most of a horse's needs for protein, vitamins and carbohydrate. However, when it is made into hay, much of the nutritional value is lost, though haylage and silage retain more 'goodness'.

This means that in winter, or at times when horses need a higher plane of nutrition, supplementary vitamins and minerals may be needed to provide an adequate intake of nutrients. These can be provided in the form of a feed supplement or a feed balancer, or can be derived from 'short feeds' or 'concentrates' – for example cereals, mixes and compounded nuts – when fed at recommended levels. Short feeds tend to contain relatively high levels of starch (carbohydrate) and give horses more energy than the fibre in forage or chaff. Energy levels can be increased further by the addition of sugar-beet pulp and vegetable oil. High fibre mixes may be used to bulk up a horse's ration and provide a 'slow-release' energy source.

Food requirements vary according to the size of a horse, its workload, and the type of food used, but the average 500kg (1,000lb) horse in medium work does well on around 7–8kg (15–18lb) forage daily, and around 2.5kg (5.5lb) hard feed. Water requirements range from around 20–90ltr (4.5–20gal)/ day, depending on the type of horse, its diet, its workload, and the weather. Water should always be provided *ad lib*, and in winter it is important always to make sure that unfrozen water is available.

Where any uncertainties exist regarding the best diet for an individual horse, particularly one that has a high level of work or an underlying disease problem, it is advisable to take advice from both vets and nutritionists at the feed companies.

■ Forage alone rarely provides a nutritional balance – the horse will need some sort of concentrate feed.

What forage should I use? Which feeding regimes are inadvisable?

Horses are 'trickle feeders', designed to spend most of their time grazing, and their digestive system works best if it is fuelled little and often. Horses do well on good quality grass as their principle form of forage, but if this is not available, most performance horses do best on haylage, which has a higher nutritional value (so less volume needs to be fed) and is less dusty than hay. When hay is fed it should be ensured that it is good quality, and reasonably fresh (much of the nutritional value fades after around six months), and if soaked to remove dust, it should only be left in water for a short period of time or some of the nutrients leach out. Concentrate feed should be fed in small amounts (preferably no more than 2kg/ 5.5lb at each feed), access to a salt/ mineral block is advisable, and fresh water should always be available.

To avoid digestive upsets and colic, horses should not be fed or watered within an hour of exercise, any changes in diet should be made gradually, and as much food as possible should be fed as forage. Feeding a forage-based diet helps keep the digestive system as healthy as possible, and also reduces the

Pasture problems

➤ Certain pasture types can be associated with health problems, and any change in the diet can cause digestive disorders, so horses should be introduced to new pastures gradually by initially limiting their time out, or by strip grazing them.
➤ Some pastures are consistently implicated in cases of grass sickness, and although we don't really understand why, it makes sense to avoid turning out horses on pastures that have previously been associated with grass sickness (Colic p102).
➤ Short grass on dry sandy soil is often associated with the development of sand colic (Colic p102), so this should also be avoided.
➤ Fast-growing spring grass and recently frosted grass may contain high levels of fructans, which can be implicated in the development of laminitis (Laminitis p122), and may also cause colic, so turning out susceptible horses and ponies in such conditions should also be avoided.

■ Good quality hay forms the forage basis for many horses' diets, but can be dusty so may need soaking before feeding.

incidence of vices (Vices p50) such as crib-biting, wind-sucking and weaving by keeping the horse occupied. A diet that is high in starch (that is, concentrates) is associated with an increased incidence of ulcers, colic (Colic p102), laminitis (Laminitis p122) and tying up (Azoturia p139). In fact, one study showed that horses fed high levels of concentrate were four times more likely to develop colic than those fed less short feed, and that changes in the diet were also associated with an increased incidence of colic. Feeding fibre sources such as chaff with short feed also aids digestion by increasing saliva production.

What nutritional requirements does my in-foal mare have?

The food requirements of a pregnant mare in the first nine months of her pregnancy are no different from the basic maintenance requirements of an adult horse, and can be met with forage and concentrates or supplements depending on the mare's condition and workload. In the last two months of pregnancy and during lactation a mare's requirements for protein and energy increase to almost double, and calcium, phosphorus and other mineral requirements also increase rapidly so that supplementary feeding is required at this time.

Throughout pregnancy and lactation, forage should be the main food source, but this can be gradually changed to alfalfa hay (which has a higher nutritional value than grass hay) or a higher energy haylage, to increase the energy and nutrient levels at this time. Concentrate feeds usually become necessary: stud mixes or stud cubes are formulated to provide the required energy and nutrients in a concentrated form so that the amount of bulk fed can be minimized.

By weaning, the foal should already be receiving much of his nutrition from creep feed and forage and so the mare's requirements gradually fall back to maintenance levels.

Maintaining an appetite in pregnancy

Ensuring sufficient nutrient intake in the last two months of pregnancy can be difficult. Try:
- ➤ using high energy forage
- ➤ adding appropriate hard feeds
- ➤ feeding four small meals daily
- ➤ adding chopped apples and carrots to make food more tasty
- ➤ damping food to increase palatability.

■ In late pregnancy a mare's food requirements increase rapidly.

How should I feed my foal to maximize his potential?

All a foal's initial feed requirements are satisfied by the mother's milk. They need to suckle within a few hours of birth, and to have fed well within 12 hours of birth, because the quality of colostrum, the mare's first milk, wanes rapidly after this time, and that first ingestion of colostrum is essential to provide a new foal with the antibodies necessary to give it immunity from ingestion of disease and infection, as well as energy. Thereafter milk normally remains the main source of energy, but creep feeding can be started from around three weeks of age (although sometimes it can be started in the first week if the mare's milk supply proves to be insufficient to meet the foal's needs).

Foals are normally weaned between four and six months of age, at which stage they are in their fastest growth phase, gaining around 1kg (2.2lb)/day. At this stage they need a concentrate feed that has higher levels of protein and minerals than their mothers generally require, as well as continued access to grass and hay or haylage. Concentrates are normally fed at a level of around 0.75–1 per cent of bodyweight daily: thus a 250kg (550lb) weanling/yearling may need around 2.5kg (5.5lb) concentrate daily. This can be continued through the first winter to help supplement winter grazing and hay with the protein and minerals that are needed for healthy growth. However, it is important to avoid foals growing too fast, or becoming overweight, so some breeds do best on a restricted energy diet.

At the age of 12 months most foals are 90 per cent of their adult height and 60 per cent of their adult weight, and are still growing fast. Between 18 months and two years their growth rate slows, and so at this stage they can gradually change to a diet that is formulated for adult horses.

Creep feeds

Creep feeds are based on milk and are thus relatively easy for the foal to digest, and together with access to hay and grass, they help to prepare its digestive system for a more adult diet, and to prevent digestive problems such as colic and diarrhoea at weaning. They also help to ensure the foal has an adequate supply of minerals (and its requirement for these is proportionally greater than its mother's), which in turn help to prevent developmental orthopaedic problems such as OCD (OCD p134).

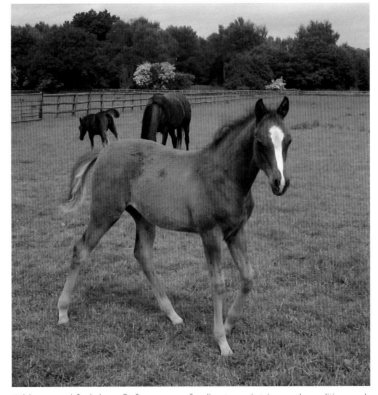

■ Unweaned foals benefit from creep feeding to maintain good condition and avoid digestive disturbances at weaning.

What diet is appropriate for my 13-year-old hack?

All horses do best on a forage-based diet, and ideally need at least 1 per cent of their bodyweight in forage daily – that is, around 5kg (11lb) for a 500kg (1,100lb) horse. This can be provided as a combination of grass and good quality hay/haylage. However, those horses that have a tendency to gain weight can have part of their forage provided as hay of lower nutritional quality (by which I mean clean but more fibrous hay, as opposed to poor quality hay with dust and fungal spores in it) or straw to reduce calorific intake.

In addition, most horses benefit from some concentrate feed to provide them with their vitamin and mineral requirements. However, those horses that are overweight may only need a low calorie nutrient supplement. Feeding short feeds or feed balancers is particularly important in the winter months, as hay has a lower nutritional quality than grass and provides fewer of the necessary nutrients. The exact choice of ration – for example, a 'cool' mix, or one for weight gain – will depend on the type of horse, its build, and the type of work it is in; but an appropriate concentrate diet (either nuts or a mix) can be fed together with chaffs/chops that aid saliva production and thus digestion, and some chopped vegetables for palatability.

Sensible use of feed supplements

Many healthy horses that are on a low or medium plane of exercise get all the nutrients they need from their forage and short feed. However, horses on restricted feed may need nutrient supplementation, as may those that exercise at a high level. Specific feed supplements may also be used to help treat horses with diseases such as arthritis, breathing problems, liver conditions and poor hoof quality.

■ Horses in light to medium work generally do well on a forage-based diet with some supplementary feeding to maintain energy levels and a nutritional balance.

I have a healthy veteran: what special feeding might he need?

Most veterans have the same food requirements as middle-aged horses, because although their ability to digest food may have reduced with age, their workload is usually lower, too. However, it is important to remember to pay close attention to the health status of veterans in case they need special feeding or management to keep them as well as possible. Regular dentistry can help maintain good tooth function, which in turn allows adequate chewing and salivation to start digestion. Blood tests can be taken to check liver and kidney function, and the general health status of the older horse in case specific treatment or maybe a special diet is necessary.

Those horses that start to lose condition can be helped by

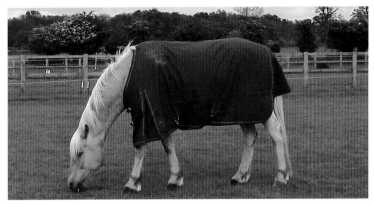

■ Rugging up helps to minimize energy wastage, and is particularly helpful in older horses.

giving high quality forage (it is important to try to keep as much as possible of the diet forage-based). High energy concentrate feeds may be used to ensure adequate mineral and vitamin levels (the absorption of these nutrients can decrease in older

horses) whilst keeping the amount of concentrates fed to a minimum. Keeping a horse well rugged up helps to minimize the amount of energy it expends in keeping warm, and this becomes particularly important for the older horse or pony.

My mare has had colic surgery: what feeding will she need now?

In the immediate aftermath of colic surgery, horses may be fed an intravenous diet or a complete liquid diet. Feeding small amounts of grass is usually started after 24 hours or so, and increased over the following few days according to appetite. If possible, in the first few weeks hay and other fibrous foods such as chaff and straw

■ A grass-based diet helps recovery from most diseases.

should be avoided, and instead the diet should be based on grass, together with soft mashes or gruels made from dried grass/ alfalfa. Concentrate feeds can be introduced in a mash form to increase the available level of nutrients: a diet that is high in protein, amino acids, vitamins B, C and E and energy helps healing, and it also helps to discourage post-operative infections.

What should I feed my show jumper?...and my endurance horse?

■ Horses in high performance work may need a diet that will give them an increase in energy levels.

Supplements for the competition animal

➤ Ensuring adequate vitamin, mineral and electrolyte intake is particularly important for horses that are working hard, so electrolyte supplements are also commonly used to counteract losses in sweat.

➤ Vitamin E and selenium supplementation can also be helpful to maintain healthy muscle and to avoid tying up (Azoturia p139), and supplementing these is particularly important if a high fat diet is being fed in order to increase energy levels in the feed.

➤ Such diets (around 10 per cent fat, supplied as vegetable oil) provide high levels of easily mobilizable energy, and can be used for horses that are doing high stamina work – for example endurance, cross-country and eventing.

Horses in high performance work may need to consume up to 3.5 per cent of their bodyweight daily in food in order to obtain sufficient nutrients. This can be hard to achieve, as some horses lose their appetite at higher planes of exercise and can then become increasingly difficult to feed. To keep energy levels high enough whilst at the same time maintaining sufficient appetite to allow intake of the desired food, forage levels are often reduced so that proportionately more concentrate feeds can be fed. However, feeding a diet too high in starch is associated with various disease problems (Diet p26), and so it is important that you try to maintain forage levels in the diet. High energy forages such as haylage and alfalfa hay are often used, so that high energy concentrates need only be fed in a relatively low volume: this should allow sufficient nutrient intake to be maintained.

Feeding increased levels of carbohydrate the night before an event helps to bind water in the lower gut and make it available during the event, thus reducing the chance of dehydration. Withholding carbohydrate on the morning of an event can also be helpful, as this aids mobilization of energy during performance. On the day of a competition, energy and fluid levels can be maintained by providing well soaked sugar beet, as both the fluid and energy sources in this feed source are readily available.

Maximizing your horse's lung capacity

The other important consideration is that it is usually a horse's breathing, rather than either his musculoskeletal fitness or energy levels, that limits his athletic performance. So at high levels of exercise it becomes particularly important to maximize the capacity of the lungs by avoiding dust in the forage and bedding.

My daughter's pony gets laminitis: what feed can he have?

Many ponies that are prone to laminitis (Laminitis p122), or that need to lose weight, do best on nothing other than restricted forage and sufficient low energy concentrate feed or food balancer to provide their nutritional requirements. The ration should be broken into many small meals daily to avoid leaving the guts empty (which increases the chance of digestive problems). Provision of probiotics to maintain a healthy balance of gut bacteria may also help to avoid laminitis. The energy levels in forage can be restricted (but not too much, or disease such as hyperlipidaemia can result: see hyperlipidaemia p109) by avoiding lush grass, by strip grazing, using a 'starvation' paddock for most of the day, or by corralling the pony for part of the day in a menage/ sand school with access to only low quality hay/ straw. Muzzling for a part of the day may also be appropriate.

It is particularly important to avoid fast-growing spring grass in conditions where low temperatures are followed by warm weather, as these conditions increase fructan levels in the grass and are associated with an increased incidence of laminitis.

If higher levels of energy are needed for performance, this can usually be achieved by improving the amount or quality of forage fed and adding fat (in the form of vegetable oil) where necessary. Where possible, concentrates (and cereals) that are high in starch should be avoided, as they are associated with increased gut fermentation and an increased incidence of laminitis.

■ Ponies that are prone to laminitis often do well on restricted rations – grazing can be limited, and part of the day spent in a sand school.

What should I feed my mare: she gets allergic skin disease?

Skin disease due to food allergies is relatively uncommon in horses, but it can occur, causing urticaria, pruritis, scurfiness and loss of hair (Skin disease p83). In most cases any allergies present are directed against cereals – wheat, barley, oats, corn – in the diet, and cutting out concentrate feeds often results in the problem being resolved. Energy can then be provided in the form of fat (horses are rarely allergic to vegetable oil), and nutrients supplemented as necessary. If this results in a resolution of the symptoms, cereals can then be added back into the diet one at a time, a new one every two weeks, to see which ones cause an adverse reaction. A feed that avoids those ingredients can then be used. Recently blood allergy tests (Allergy tests p81) have been developed that can also give information concerning which food ingredients horses are sensitive to, and this can help when you are planning a diet for susceptible horses.

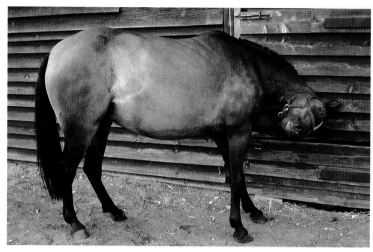

■ Horses with allergic skin disease may need to try a low allergy diet, or an exclusion diet.

My gelding has been diagnosed with liver disease: what can I feed him?

Horses with liver disease often suffer additional problems (Liver disease p109) such as weight loss, diarrhoea, and even neurological problems, but these can be addressed by manipulating their diet. It is important to provide feed that is palatable (these horses often have a reduced appetite), and in several small meals daily to maintain a low level of gut fill. The diet should be relatively low in protein, but should provide good quality protein that is high in short-branched chain amino acids (soybean and linseed can help achieve this) to reduce the liver's workload. Levels of fat in the diet should be kept low to prevent hyperlipidaemia (Hyperlipidaemia p109), and salt levels should also be kept as low as possible. However, starchy foods can be used to provide energy and nutrients, and supplementation, particularly of the B vitamins and also vitamin E, is advisable.

Affected horses may have increased water requirements, so it is very important to ensure that clean and fresh water is always available. In winter, water can be warmed so that intake is not reduced because the horse finds extremely cold water unpalatable.

Horses that have diarrhoea do best if starchy foods are avoided, and they also benefit from an easily digestible, forage-based diet, together with adequate nutrient supplementation and added probiotics.

My old mare's teeth are worn: how can I help her to gain weight?

When trying to keep old, thin horses in good condition, it is important to maximize their chances of maintaining weight by cutting down on energy losses – for instance, by rugging them effectively to prevent energy being lost as heat – and by keeping their digestive function as good as possible with regular dentistry and worming. The most important factor for horses with poor teeth is to ensure that they get good quality dental care at least twice yearly to maximize their ability to chew (Dentistry p15); otherwise the digestibility of the forage they do manage to swallow is reduced, as is its effective nutritional value to that horse. Regular, gentle exercise can also help maintain appetite and digestive function, but higher exercise levels that utilize increased energy should be avoided. In addition, it is advisable to have a veterinary check to ensure there is no underlying disease that requires specific treatment.

Given that the horse is otherwise well, weight can be maintained or built up using good quality forage and a high energy, easily digestible concentrate feed fed in several – for example, six – meals daily. Grass is the easiest and most natural

■ Even with supplementary feeding, it can be difficult to keep sufficient weight on some older horses.

forage for a horse to get into its mouth and chew, so as much of the diet as possible should be provided as good quality grass. Dried grass, grass nuts and alfalfa cubes can be used to make mashes that are easy to eat and provide fibre-based energy, and easily digestible short chops can also be used. Alfalfa/ alfalfa hay can be used as it is of relatively high nutritional value, *except for* older horses that might have kidney disease as it could exacerbate such a condition.

A variety of commercial mixes are available that are specially formulated for geriatrics, to help weight gain. Dampening such feeds makes them softer and easier to chew, and rolled or mashed cereals as well as fat (vegetable oil) and well soaked sugar beet can be used to provide easily available energy (though a high fat diet should be avoided if there are any signs of liver disease (Hyperlipidaemia p109)). It is important to ensure sufficient intake of nutrients, and to provide a salt lick to ensure adequate salt levels.

How can I avoid lameness and other diseases occurring during exercise?

The best way to avoid lameness occurring during exercise is to ensure that the horse is fit and used to the level of exercise expected of it. Accidents and injuries generally happen when horses are tired, and don't take so much care about where they put their feet as a consequence, or when their tendons, ligaments and muscles are working beyond their usual range of exercise and are thus more subject to stresses and strains.

It is advisable, therefore, to make sure horses and ponies are exercised regularly through the week (ideally at least four out of the seven days), and that their fitness is maintained at a level sufficient to prepare them for their workload. For instance, you can't expect children's ponies to stand in the field doing nothing during the whole of the term-time and then perform at Pony Club events all holidays without preparation, any more than you would expect your horse (or yourself!) to do an endurance ride without first building up its (or your!) fitness.

As well as ensuring sufficient fitness, the avoidance of accidents, injuries and disease also involves using appropriate tack, making sure the feet are properly trimmed (Farriery p16), using level ground where possible, ensuring that horses are well handled and confident in their surroundings, and keeping to a speed that is appropriate to the going and the environment.

In the winter, clipping helps to prevent both excessive fluid losses in sweat, and skin irritation. Also studs may be needed in snowy, muddy or very dry conditions to help traction and reduce the chance of injuries.

■ It is important to build up fitness gradually before attempting high levels of exercise.

How much exercise does a horse or pony need and how much of it ridden?

The level and type of exercise that a horse needs depends on many factors. In order to reduce the risk of injuries (Lameness p119) it is important to ensure fitness through regular ridden (or driven) work, lungeing, in-hand exercise, or exercise on a horse-walker. Exercise also fulfils an important psychological role for horses and ponies – exercise at liberty in the field, in particular, helps to prevent vices (Vices p50) and bad behaviour, because horses that spend long periods of time stabled can become bored, stressed and unhappy. Ideally all horses should be turned out for part of every day, and horses in work should be exercised at least four days a week.

■ Using a horse-walker is an easy way to maintain fitness for the owner with limited time to give their horse regular work.

know-how: Developing safe exercise regimes

Planning a suitable exercise regime requires careful thought and its execution necessitates commitment to regular riding. It may be necessary to start building fitness 2–3 months before a planned event to ensure that a horse will be able to cope. Specific exercise regimes depend on the age and build of the horse and his type of work, however most are broadly similar.

WEEKS 1–4
- Build strength and muscle with walking exercise increasing from half an hour to two hours daily.
- Exercise at least four days a week to maintain a low level of fitness and six days a week to build it up for events.
- Hill work, lungeing and long reining can all aid muscle development.

WEEKS 5–8
- Add and build up periods of trot to help strengthen the limbs.
- Then introduce canter to aid cardiovascular fitness and build muscle strength.
- Schooling and lateral work helps build up specific muscle groups.

- Work over poles and low jumps aids coordination and limb strength.
- Ensure a minimum of 15 minutes walking 'warm up' and 'cool down' time.

WEEKS 9–12 & BEYOND
- 2–3 sessions a week of galloping or interval training (alternate periods of canter and walk) can be introduced to develop stamina.
- Jumping can be increased as coordination and strength improve.
- Small competitions can be incorporated into the schedule to maintain motivation and interest.
- Short breaks can allow a horse to remain fresh without dropping fitness.

WARNING SIGNS OF OVERWORK
- Back pain and subtle lamenesses often manifested as poor performance or a disunited canter.
- Limb swellings and areas of heat can indicate an incipient problem.
- Noisy or disrupted breathing, coughing and nosebleeds relate to poor lung performance.
- Heart rates normally rise from around 30bpm to 100–160 during fast work. This value should drop below 64bpm within 10 minutes of work ceasing. Sustained high heart rates indicate lack of fitness or a heart problem.

How do I build up fitness while avoiding illness?

Any exercise regime that builds up stamina and speed gradually will allow fitness to develop to a level suitable for the exercise required of the horse, thus helping to avoid disease.

DEVELOPING MUSCLE

It is important to bear in mind that fitness involves developing muscle, tendon, ligament and bone strength and mobility as well as improving heart and lung function, and all these systems work best if they are built up gradually to the required level and type of exercise.

REGIMES FOR YOUNG HORSES OR THOSE RETURNING TO WORK

Whether bringing on a young horse, or a horse that has been unwell or out of work (Exercise regimes

■ Long-reining helps to build fitness, and can be particularly useful for young horses.

p37), the basic principle is the same: to build fitness, horses need regular work most days of the week, and they need to increase the level of performance attained and the duration of exercise gradually.

Most horses do well starting with several months of mainly walking exercise. They can then progress to increasing periods of trot, which help to reduce excess fat, build up topline muscles and strength, and prepare the heart and lungs for more demanding levels of exercise.

Short periods of faster work can be introduced as fitness improves and other types of exercise such as swimming and work over jumps can help maintain variety.

What exercise regime is suitable for a horse that has had a tendon injury?

After tendon and ligament injuries (Tendon injuries p128) it is usually advisable to have an initial period of box rest (often one to three months) while the primary phase of healing takes place. Once there is ultrasonographic (Ultrasonography p129) evidence of sufficient healing, a period of gradually increasing exercise is advisable to improve the strength of the healed tendon/ ligament; a typical regime would involve a period of controlled exercise each day, and the rest of the time the horse would be kept in its box or 'playpen'.

It is usually advisable to start with about 10–15 minutes walking exercise daily (either in hand or with a light rider), and then to increase this by about five minutes each week as long as there is no sign of the injury taking a turn for the worse – that is, as long as there is no evidence of heat, pain, swelling or lameness. Repeat ultrasonography can be used to monitor the healing process, and after one to two months the period of exercise may include a short spell of trot, initially at five minutes daily, which may then be increased by approximately five minutes each week. Once the horse can do around 30 minutes of trot daily it will probably be able to withstand the stresses of uncontrolled turnout, and so it can be turned out in the field; but the exercise regime should continue to be built up gradually over the subsequent couple of months or so, to full speed and jumping.

■ Restricting a horse that has had a tendon injury to a 'playpen' can be helpful during the recovery period.

How can I get my son's laminitic pony well enough to work?

Ponies (and horses) with laminitis (Laminitis p122) need to be treated very carefully in order to avoid their condition being exacerbated to a point where they can no longer recover. It is therefore important to take signs of laminitis very seriously, and to monitor ponies that are prone to laminitis very carefully on a daily basis. Any signs of heat in the feet, an increased digital pulse (How to check the digital pulse p124) or lameness should be treated immediately with box rest, and prompt veterinary advice should be sought. Ponies with laminitis should be box rested until they are sound (and off medication), at which point their exercise should be built up gradually. Work involving high levels of concussion, on roads and hard ground, should be avoided as this can cause laminitis. It is important not to attempt higher levels of exercise (for instance, Pony Club) without a period of building up exercise. Keeping the weight of laminitic ponies under control,

and their exercise regular, is of paramount importance in maintaining them as ponies that can continue to work.

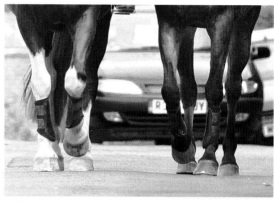

■ Controlling weight through exercise is important for laminitis-prone horses and ponies, but the concussive nature of roadwork means that it should be avoided.

Can you give me some advice about safety on the road?

Around six riders and even more horses are killed every year on roads in the UK, and higher numbers in the USA. It therefore makes sense to avoid roads, and to keep to bridleways and paths where this is practicable. It is important to make sure that horses are used to traffic, and are controllable on the roads, so they are never responsible for causing an accident. Visibility should be maximized with stirrup lights and reflective coats, saddlecloths and boots. Also, riding on roads should be avoided at times when visibility for drivers is difficult (such as early mornings and evenings, and at night).

■ Take responsibility for making you and your horse visible to other road users. Reflective coats and strips that can be attached to bandages and tack help to make you both more visible.

Field safety

Safety in the stable

Safety away from home

What is the safest fencing available; and do I have to use post and rails?

To be safe, fencing needs to be well maintained, strong, easily visible and also high enough to dissuade horses from attempting to jump it. However, even certain types of fencing that fulfil these criteria are regularly associated with injuries, the most common of these being barbed wire, which very readily can cause cuts and grazes if horses lean on to it, back up to it, or get tangled in it. Stock fencing can also cause problems as horses can get their feet stuck in it, although its use may be advisable in areas of the USA where opossums are implicated in spreading equine protozooal myeloencephalitis (Neurological disease p140) and need to be kept out of fields. Any fencing that has worked itself loose, or is looped at or near ground level, or is damaged, constitutes a risk, and

■ Post and rail fencing can always be combined with stock-proof fencing if necessary.

a potential hazard on which horses may injure themselves.

Horses should be introduced to new pastures in hand, and hand grazed until they settle down. In addition, horses should always be introduced to electric fencing carefully to avoid panic and subsequent injuries.

■ Electric tape can provide a safe alternative to post and rail fencing and cannot be chewed like wooden fencing can.

Avoiding injuries from fencing

➤ Injuries most commonly happen when horses are introduced to a new field where the fencing is not clearly visible; when new horses are added to a group and individuals become over-excited; or when horses get into conflict near a fence.

➤ Where wire fencing is used it can be made more obvious with plastic markers – for instance, pieces of plastic bag tied on to the fence. Generally either post and rail fencing or electric tape fencing are the most practical and safe forms of fencing, particularly when combined with hedging, although even these can cause problems occasionally.

➤ Putting up fencing so that it doesn't make a corner anywhere, where horses can be trapped and risk coming into conflict with others, and double fencing between groups of horses, will minimize injury.

What kind of pasture will suit my horse best?

The kind of pasture that will suit a given group of horses or ponies best depends on their type and workload. Obviously small ponies that are prone to laminitis do best on a relatively poor pasture, whilst performance horses do best on good quality grass as the basis for their diet. To maximize the quality of grass, it is important to ensure that the pasture is seeded with a good mix of meadow grasses, herbs and other plants. Horses should be moved on to fresh pastures gradually (by time restriction or strip grazing) to prevent digestive problems (Feeding p23). Fields should be adequately rested. Soil testing and appropriate fertilization may be needed to maintain grass quality, but fertilized pastures must be rested for the prescribed period of time before horses or ponies are returned to graze them, to avoid them coming into contact with potentially toxic chemicals. Regular harrowing and rolling can also help stimulate grass growth.

Dung collection should ideally be carried out on a daily basis so as to reduce the exposure of horses to worms (Worms p17), and to maximize the areas of grass that the horses consider edible, otherwise they will tend to avoid large areas of 'roughs' where they have defecated. Any ragwort coming up should be pulled regularly before it seeds (Ragwort p108): this is far more effective and less dangerous than spraying. Removal of wilted plants is also important, as ragwort may become more palatable as it dries. Other poisonous plants should be removed or fenced off, and any large areas of nettles should also be removed, as nettle stings have the potential to cause horses to collapse.

What risks are there in fields that I need to be aware of?

Apart from the risks posed by inappropriate fencing, there are certain other hazards that owners should look out for, and it is important to walk new fields and examine them carefully. Dangers include old coils of wire fencing, old agricultural equipment, and batteries that may be hidden in long grass. Other risks include glass and construction waste, and damaged shelters, water tanks and food racks. Holes, ditches, ponds and rabbit warrens can also cause injury, and should be removed, filled in, or fenced off.

It is important that horses have thick hedges, substantial trees or, more preferably, buildings to provide shelter in their field against both sunshine and bad weather. Field shelters should be well constructed and in good repair. They should stand out of the muddy areas of the field and open away from the prevailing wind. Hay racks, feed troughs or bowls and water tanks should also be well maintained, clean, and safe, and it is important to ensure that there is sufficient access to hay, food and water so that horses don't end up fighting for it.

All horses at pasture should be checked at least twice daily so that any injuries or problems are identified promptly.

■ Loose wire should be removed or tightened up; and ideally something other than barbed wire should be used as fencing material.

What poisonous plants do I need to look out for?

Although generally horses won't eat poisonous plants unless they are really hungry, there are occasional incidences of them 'getting a taste' for something that is bad for them, so their sense of taste can't be relied upon to prevent poisoning. It is therefore important to remove or fence off all poisonous plants, and to check fields regularly for new plants, and also for householders' garden waste (especially grass clippings), any of which can cause problems. Poisonous plants that are removed should be burnt in order to prevent horses having further access to them.

The most significant plant poisonous to horses is undoubtedly ragwort (Ragwort p108), which causes liver disease and death in large numbers of horses every year. The importance of removing it – alive and, even more especially, dead when it is in fact more toxic – from fields cannot be over-emphasized. Acorns from oak trees, and yew can also be fatal – acorns are extremely palatable to horses, and can cause kidney failure (Kidney disease p111), whilst even a small amount of yew can be immediately toxic, and cause heart failure (Heart disease p93).

Other plants that are particularly dangerous include bracken and laburnum, both of which can cause neurological symptoms (Neurological disease p140) such as shaking, staggering, dribbling, collapse and death. A range of other plants can also cause illness: these include avocado, privet, bryony, bog asphodel, nightshade, oleander, charlock, hemlock, horse chestnuts, horsetail, monkshood, cowbane, St John's wort, foxgloves, rhododendron, pokeweed, locoweed, yellow star thistle, poppies, and even potato plants. In the USA, in particular, red maple is also a significant risk, as horses will sometimes eat the leaves when they fall, and even a small amount can result in anaemia (Anaemia p141) and can be potentially fatal.

Initially poisoning is usually characterized by either neurological symptoms, or colic (Colic p61, 102) or diarrhoea (Diarrhoea p105), but symptoms can develop further and prove fatal. Consumption of toxic plants by pregnant mares can be particularly problematic, and may result in foetal deformities and abortion (Reproductive disease p114); it is therefore particularly important that pregnant mares are kept on safe pastures.

Note that in the UK, the 1959 Weed Act makes it an offence to allow ragwort to spread. A similar law applies in many US states.

know-how: Poisonous plant identifier

It is worth taking a few minutes to memorize the appearance of some of the more common poisonous plants so that they can be identified promptly and access to them can be prevented.

■ Ragwort   ■ Yew   ■ Laburnum   ■ Oak   ■ Red maple

My horse gets sunburn: can it be avoided and is it a sign of liver failure?

Any areas of skin that are unpigmented – white – can become sunburnt, and those that have little hair to protect them are most at risk. This means that white areas on the nose, face and ears are particularly prone to sunburn (Skin disease p83), and raw, crusty lesions can easily develop in the summer months, particularly in areas of strong sunshine. Sunburn also commonly affects white skin on the lower limbs, and can be part of a syndrome involving inflammation and infection of the skin in the fetlock and pastern area; other contributing causes include tick bites, mud fever and lower limb injuries.

Those conditions that cause photosensitization make horses more susceptible to sunburn. Liver disease (Liver disease p109) can result in increased skin levels of photoactive toxins produced by plant digestion (one of the functions of the healthy liver is to

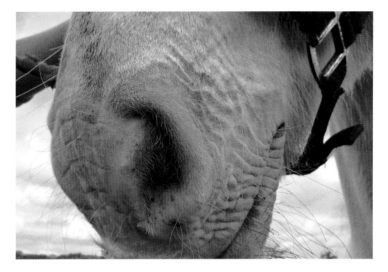

detoxify such chemicals), and these chemicals cause an excessive reaction to sunlight, with increased levels of inflammation and sunburn. Even in normal horses, certain plants – for example St John's Wort, buckwheat, various brassicas in large quantities, charlock, ragwort and bog asphodel – release high levels of photoactive

■ Sunburn is a particular problem for horses with unpigmented skin on their faces and limbs.

chemicals and these can cause photosensitization. There are certain types of medication that may also be implicated.

Photosensitizing plants should be avoided where possible, and liver disease treated promptly to avoid such problems. Sunburn is obviously best avoided by preventing the sun reaching unpigmented areas by not turning the horse or pony out during the brightest, sunniest hours of the day (though this doesn't stop them getting sunburnt faces if they look out over their stable doors), by using light summer sheets, and by using high-factor waterproof sunblock every day on exposed, unpigmented skin.

■ Plants such as St John's Wort (used to treat depression in humans) can cause photosensitization and sunburn in horses.

How can I avoid my horse getting bullied in the field?

A common cause of injury is a horse being kicked in the field following some equine dispute. This generally happens in multi-owner livery yards, where large numbers of horses are turned out in the same field, and where conflict over any number of issues can occur. Usually the problem involves competition over food, hay, water, grazing or shade, so in order to avoid conflict be sure there is plenty to go round, and that supplies of these items are well spread out. Fencing fields so that they have curved corners can also be helpful, as it prevents submissive horses from getting stuck in a corner when they want to get out of the way, and double fencing between different groups of horses – particularly mares and colts or geldings – also helps to prevent horses becoming over-excited and lashing out.

Horses do best in relatively small but stable groups, in which they can work out a fair pecking order and then accept it. It is rare for dominant horses to terrorize others, and disputes don't usually happen once the hierarchy is sorted out. However, particularly dominant or aggressive horses will sometimes consistently pick on others and cause injury, and if this situation does not resolve, the only option may be to remove the bully from the group.

In most cases, though, few problems occur as long as horses are allowed to sort themselves out – intervening in an equine dispute generally achieves very little, other than putting the person at risk. Introducing a new horse to an established group, however, is always a risky time and one when fights can occur; it is often a good idea to give the group a chance to get used to the new horse by initially turning him out in a neighbouring field.

■ Horses and ponies do best turned out in familiar groups.

Is it really necessary to keep mares and geldings separate?

In small, stable groups of horses it is not always necessary to separate them according to gender. However, where horses are kept in larger groups and new horses are introduced from time to time, there is far more likelihood of conflicts occurring, and this is only exacerbated by mixing mares and geldings.

When 'in season', mares are far more likely to kick and injure other horses. This is exacerbated by the presence of male horses, which tend to get too close and consequently invite injury. Even geldings may show an interest in 'in season' mares, as, despite being castrated, they retain some of the male hormones that control behaviour. To avoid highly charged, hormonally driven situations occurring, it is therefore sensible to keep mares and geldings separate and to pasture them apart with a double fence between.

■ Mares and geldings can bond well in small groups.

What are the best stabling systems, and why?

There are a number of different ways to design stables for horses, and as long as the basic requirements are met, the details are not too important. Whether farm buildings are converted into stalls or loose boxes, stable blocks are constructed, or Dutch barns containing loose boxes are built, probably the single most important factor from a medical point of view is that good ventilation is ensured. The main limiting factor of a horse's athletic performance is his breathing (Respiratory disease p96), and even low levels of dust or cobwebs can contribute to reduced respiratory function. Ideally, therefore, all stables should have windows opening to the outside, even if they also open into a covered barn area. Because the barn system comprises a shared airspace, any straw or hay that is stored, used as bedding, or fed to any of the horses in the barn, may cause dust to affect other horses even if they themselves are managed on low-dust bedding and dust-free/ soaked hay. Many yards therefore choose to bed all their horses on shavings, paper, card or other low-dust bedding and to feed them all on dust-free forage.

The barn system allows for a high degree of socialization between horses in adjacent loose boxes, which helps to keep them occupied. This usually reduces the occurrence of vices (Vices p50), except when horses that dislike each other are stabled side by side, which can result in increased stress to one or both of them. By contrast, conventional stables generally don't allow for a shared airspace, and don't usually have windows that bring horses into direct contact; thus the closest that stabled horses usually get to one another is when they have their head out over the door. As this prevents much socialization, it can be associated with more vices.

Other factors that are important in the construction of good stables are that they are of solid construction and well maintained, so as to prevent injuries; that they are appropriately drained so that the beds are easy to keep dry and clean; and that electric supplies are protected, and of appropriate (non-domestic) construction. Smoking and other sources of fire should be banned from stable and barn areas.

■ Stables should be well constructed and have good ventilation.

What bedding materials are available, and what should I use?

A variety of bedding materials is available for horses, and the one you choose will inevitably depend to some extent on cost, as well as what the horse is used for, and the health of its respiratory system.

The cleanliness and dryness of the bed is of particular importance if horses have any injuries that could become contaminated by dirty bedding, and at such times beds should be mucked out as often as is necessary to keep them clean. Ideally wounds should be covered in order to prevent contamination. Most types of bedding material may be eaten by some individuals, and they should be stopped from doing this, otherwise impaction colic (Colic p102) may result.

When choosing a bedding material, it may also be important to consider disposal. Straw, cardboard, paper and Aubiose all rot down reasonably rapidly; shavings and pelleted wood can take a little longer. All burn reasonably well if muck heaps are to be managed by burning (though the environmental implications of this should be considered), and all are relatively easy to handle.

■ Good quality straw is appropriate for many horses in well ventilated stables, but lower dust alternatives can be used.

know-how: *Choose the right bedding*

Do you know which bedding is suitable for your horse? You may have to experiment to find one which suits both your horse and your pocket.

■ **Straw** remains commonly used, and for many horses is adequate. However, inevitably it is dusty and may compromise the performance of even those horses that don't have an obvious cough, and therefore many owners choose to use bedding that is less dusty.

■ **Shavings** are relatively low in dust, work very well, and, like straw, tend to keep the top surface of the bed reasonably dry as fluids drain down.

■ **Paper and cardboard** can also be used, but paper in particular tends to cause a lot of mess as it gets blown around a yard, and both paper and cardboard tend to soak in moisture rather than wick it away, and so result in a wetter bed.

■ **Pelleted wood and Aubiose** are low-dust alternatives that are being increasingly used, as they provide a comfortable and supportive bed (the latter is a particularly important quality for laminitics).

■ **Sand** can also provide a comfortable and supportive bedding material for laminitics.

■ **Rubber mats** are used in many stables, either under a small amount of another bedding material, or alone. However, few horses will choose to lie down on a bed that is rubber matting alone, as it is somewhat cold and can get dirty. Ideally horses should have a warm, deep bed overlying such a product.

What medical problems do vices cause? How can I prevent them?

Horses may develop a number of vices, all of which tend to relate to stress and boredom in the first instance, but which can rapidly become 'learned' behaviour that is very difficult, if not impossible, to change.

A high concentrate diet can be implicated in causing vices, but they are most commonly seen in horses that spend large amounts of time in their stables, and which don't have enough to occupy them.

The most common vices include weaving (which probably relates in greatest measure to frustrated athletic activity, as the normal horse would move around constantly as he grazes), crib-biting and wind-sucking (which probably relate to frustrated feeding activity), wood

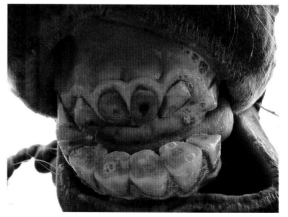

■ An anti-weaving grille (*above*) fitted to a stable door.

■ Horses that crib-bite and wind-suck (*left*) wear down their teeth, which can predispose to digestive problems. It also makes it impossible to estimate age by tooth examination (*below*).

■ A cribbing strap (*above*) can prevent crib-biting and wind-sucking.

■ Sufficient turnout and the provision of toys (*right*) helps to prevent boredom and avoid vices.

chewing, headshaking, and forms of behaviour that can cause self-injury, ranging from stamping and door kicking to flank chewing. Masturbation can also be seen in some males (both entire and gelded). These types of behaviour generally arise as the horse seeks a way to deal with stress: performing the vice comes to be a 'comforter', and the activity results in the release of stress-relieving chemicals in the brain so that the horse becomes 'addicted' to the behaviour.

Whilst keeping horses happy and occupied helps to prevent unwanted behaviour patterns developing, treating them once they have occurred is rather more difficult. However, it is most important to address such vices because, if unchecked, they can lead to limb injuries (Lameness p119), tooth injuries (Dentistry p15), an increased incidence of colic (Colic p102), weight loss (Weight loss p107), self-injury, and reduced performance. Weaving can be prevented using weaving grills, whilst crib-biting and wind-sucking can be stopped using cribbing straps, Cribbox (and other unpleasant-tasting products) and the use of electric tape to prevent access to fencing and doors on which the horse would otherwise bite. Muzzling or the use of a cradle can prevent flank chewing.

However, simply preventing these behaviour patterns is often counterproductive, as it takes away the horse's way of dealing with stress. More recent treatments that may be helpful in some cases include the use of certain foods and medicines that may help to relieve the underlying stress, and so reduce the horse's 'need' to perform these self-indulgent vice behaviours.

Measures to keep horses occupied

➤ Increasing the forage content of the diet so that horses can trickle feed, as this suits them best;

➤ turning horses out for as much of the time as possible.

➤ feeding their hay or haylage through a small-holed net or even two nets (one inside the other) to increase the time taken feeding;

➤ providing distractions in the stable such as horseballs and toys that slowly release food;

➤ maximizing horses' contact with others (as long as they are not afraid of the horses they are in contact with). Grilled windows or partitions between stables allow social contact between stabled horses.

➤ Where this is not possible or practicable, mirrors in a stable – though obviously, not glass ones – can also be helpful.

All trips away from home should start with familiarizing the horse with the vehicle and with the sensation of travelling. Even if a horse doesn't go to shows and events, it is a good idea to try and make sure that he is a confident traveller, and to take him for the occasional trip so that should he have to be taken, say, to a veterinary referral centre in an emergency, he will be better able to cope with such a journey without making his injuries or illness worse because of the additional stress from travelling.

A young horse can be familiarized with a lorry or trailer by feeding him on the ramp/inside, and gradually building up his confidence in entering a confined space, being tied up, and having the ramp put up. This will help to prevent him feeling undue alarm and panic, with the risk of potential injury. Take him on a short trip in order to build up his confidence further – with careful driving, exciting destinations and plenty of treats, most horses will come to enjoy travelling.

When planning a journey to a show or an event, it is important to make sure that you prepare for any eventuality: the potential for accidents and injuries is huge! Obviously the trailer/lorry should be well maintained and clean, with a non-slip floor and bedding. Check that the windows and ventilators work, that the partitions and walls are well padded, and that there are no sharp edges or broken or bent bits of metal that could cause

Essential items to take on board when you travel

➤ Appropriate emergency equipment, including first aid kits for both humans and horses;
➤ a mobile phone;
➤ extra rugs, bedding, food and water (some horses will only drink familiar water) for the horses, and blankets, food and water for the humans in case of breakdown, emergencies or bad weather;
➤ ice scrapers, sand and tyre chains.
➤ If travelling abroad, be sure that all the necessary paperwork (including shipping documents and proof of ID) has been completed, and that horses have had the necessary vaccinations, health certification and, in some cases, blood tests. Local authorities and vets should be able to advise as to what is required, depending on the destination. Always take the horses' passports with proof of vaccinations.

injuries. The route should be planned carefully, with places for fuel stops where the horses can be watered and fed at least every two hours; a list and details of livery yards and vets along the way can be helpful.

Before loading, it is important to make sure that the box is well prepared, and that the horse is properly protected with tail guard, leg boots, poll guard and travelling rug (unless it is hot).

Loading a horse should be straightforward if he is confident and familiar with the procedure. However, this can be a difficult time, with the potential for injury to both human and horse, so it is important to be careful. Have a secure bridle or head-collar on the horse for loading, and try to walk him straight on with confidence. Fear of confinement, separation from his friends, and the sensation, noise and smell of travelling can lead a horse to be afraid of loading, and this can be habit-forming. A bucket of food can be used to encourage him to load, and putting a travelling companion on first can be helpful. If necessary, hoods, blinkers or even a whip can be used during loading, and in some cases a lunge-line or an 'easy-loader' strap can help — although horses can still panic and risk injuring themselves or their handlers.

During travel, whether by road, rail, air or sea, one of the biggest risks is that the horse will get overheated and/ or dehydrated. Regular stops for watering and rest are therefore advisable, and electrolytes may also need to be given. Unfamiliar travellers, horses with injuries, and older horses may also have difficulty bracing themselves, particularly during a long journey. Over-tiredness can cause loss of balance, panic, and even falls and it is therefore most

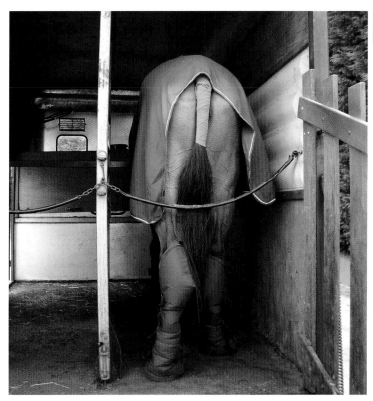

■ Horses should be familiarized with loading to prevent injuries.

important to ensure that injured limbs are well supported, and that horses have enough room and sufficient bedding. Also, plan adequate rest stops, and where necessary unload horses and give them a chance to move around and graze for a short time before re-loading and continuing a journey. Occasionally the kindest alternative is to travel an old or injured horse loose in a large compartment so that it can find its most comfortable position.

Horses should be monitored carefully both during and after travelling: sometimes 'shipping fever' (Respiratory disease p96), characterized by a cough and high temperature, may follow long distance travel. Once at a show, ensure that the tack is safe and secure, that horses are securely tied up when not being held, and that they are handled carefully. Keep mares that are in season away from other horses,

and bear in mind that any horse or pony's behaviour may be different and more difficult when away from home, and that this could well lead to kicks and injuries. When competing, it is important not to attempt to do things that the horse (or rider!) isn't up to, because this is when injuries commonly occur. Also, horses should be checked regularly, and if any signs of injury, lameness, heat, pain or swelling are seen, advice from the on-course or local veterinary surgeon should be sought, and the horse withdrawn from competition if necessary.

Trips out can be great fun for both horse and owner, but they do require a great deal of care and preparation if accidents and injuries are to be avoided.

See the Horserace Betting Levy Board's *Guidelines on the Transport of Horses* for further information (Contacts p150).

What should I have in my first aid kit, and why?

When emergencies happen, it is a good idea to have ready an easily portable kit that contains exactly the things that you might need in order to deal with the problem in the first instance. Any medicines that have been dispensed for a particular horse by the vet should be kept locked away in a box or cupboard, but a first aid kit should be accessible – not locked away – and in an easily portable box. It should be well stocked with the items listed at right (and any others you think appropriate), and checked regularly to ensure that it is always ready for action. And it is always a good idea to have access to a charged-up mobile phone when horses are around.

A first aid kit should contain:

- the vet's phone number;
- paper and pen/pencil for taking notes or writing down instructions;
- a torch;
- a spare headcollar/lead rope;
- wire cutters;
- scissors;
- tweezers;
- a clean bowl;
- some sterile syringes for flushing, and sterile water/saline;
- antiseptic spray/solution at appropriate dilution;
- fly repellent;
- sterile gel such as Intrasite for packing clean open wounds to prevent bacterial proliferation;
- petroleum jelly;
- dressings: cotton wool for cleaning wounds; Animalintex or equivalent for poulticing; sterile non-adherent dressings;
- selection of medical bandages: cotton wool-type bandage for padding, or Gamgee; elastic net type for holding dressings and padding in place; stretchy self-adherent bandage for top layer;
- sticky tape;
- tail bandages (widely useful).

How do I examine my horse for signs of disease?

Some injuries are obviously serious and it is clear that the vet should be called immediately: having a detailed look at the horse before calling the vet will merely waste valuable time, although an examination may be carried out while awaiting the vet's arrival. Other injuries can be more difficult to assess, and a good look at the horse may be needed first before a decision can be made as to the best course of action. However, it is most important to remember that horses, and particularly unwell horses, are dangerous and unpredictable, and no attempt should be made to examine a horse if to do so would put anyone at risk.

If an examination is to take place it is important to be methodical, so that you don't miss anything. The first thing to do is to check the horse's heart and breathing rates, and this should be done as quickly and calmly as possible, because examining a frightened or injured horse can cause an increase in these values. Pain, fear, some injuries and high temperatures can also increase these values.

The Normal Vital Signs

The normal vital signs of an adult horse are:

- **Temperature:** 99.8–100.5°F (37.6–38°C)
- **Pulse:** 25–40 beats/minute
- **Respiration:** 12–20 breaths/minute

A foal's values can be more varied.

A thorough and systematic approach to examining your horse helps you to avoid missing important signs or symptoms of disease.

- **The heart rate** can be felt by placing a hand on the skin just behind the left elbow, or the pulse (which normally reflects the heart rate) can be taken by placing a finger gently but firmly over the facial artery (that runs in a groove just behind the corner of the eye) or the maxillary artery (as it crosses the angle of the jaw) (*below*). A normal resting heart rate is around 25–40 beats/ minute.

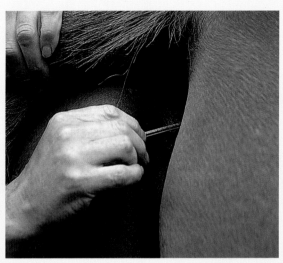

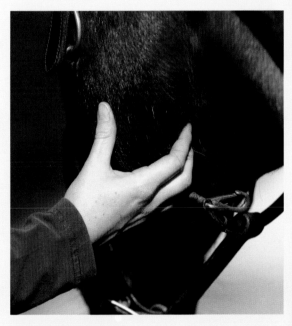

problems that can occur in severe conditions such as serious colics. Blanching the gum with the pressure of a fingertip should remove the colour for 1–3 seconds only (*below*). Any prolongation of this value would also indicate circulatory problems.

- **The breathing rate** can be counted by watching the rise and fall of the chest wall. A normal respiration rate is approximately 12–20 breaths/ minute.

- **Taking the temperature** can be a useful next step. A rectal thermometer should be inserted approximately 5cm (2in) into the rectum and held to one side (to ensure contact with the rectal wall) for 30–60 seconds (*top right*). The horse's normal temperature is 99.8–100.5°F (37.6–38°C) but is increased in infection or if the horse is otherwise in pain.

- Next, **check the circulation** in the mucous membranes by lifting a lip and looking at the colour of the gums: they should be pale pink. A dark red, purplish or greying gum indicates circulatory

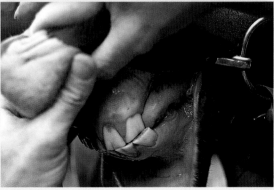

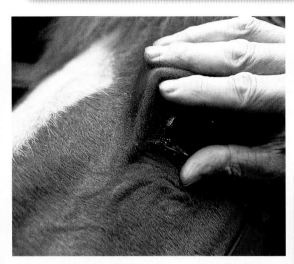

apparent depth. Any wound that is bleeding profusely or is in the vicinity of a joint or the tendons should be seen promptly by a vet.

• After that, **check the abdomen**: particularly in cases of colic, it can be useful to place an ear to either side of the tummy and listen for 'gurgley' gut sounds. An absence of these can indicate that the guts are not working properly, or that the horse is in severe pain.

• Next, **check the eyes** (*above*): are they injured in any way? Are they both clear and responsive to light (do the pupils – the black stripes across the middle of each eye – get smaller if a bright light is shone on them?), and touch (does the horse blink if you touch the lid at the corner of his eye?). Eye injuries or abnormalities always necessitate prompt veterinary attention.

• Then **look at the skin**: check all over for lumps and bumps, grazes and scrapes. If possible make a list of any injuries so that they don't get missed or forgotten, and assess each one in terms of its position (is it near a joint? or tendons?), and

• And finally, **look at the limbs**: are there any obvious areas of pain/ swelling? Can the horse bear weight on them? Any suspected joint injuries or fractures should be seen promptly, and any horse with lameness should be seen as soon as possible.

How do I stop a distressed horse injuring itself further?

While awaiting the vet, it can be helpful to restrain a frightened or panicky horse to prevent it causing itself further injury, and it will help the vet to do their job if the horse can be adequately restrained during examination. However, no attempt should be made to approach a horse if to do so would put your own, or anyone else's, safety at risk. Sometimes it is best simply to get the horse into a stable and shut the doors in the hope that it will quieten down, particularly if attempts to restrain or examine it only cause further panic and injury.

Possible methods of restraint include getting a headcollar and lead-rope or bridle on to a horse that is loose. Looping the lead-rope around the nose below the noseband may also help to restrain him, as can holding up a limb, holding on to a fold of skin on the horse's neck, or applying a twitch to its nose. Holding or twitching an ear (or the tongue) is not advisable, as this can easily cause permanent damage. If a horse is down on the ground, and it is in its best interests that it remains so, its attempts to get up can be prevented by kneeling on its head or upper neck. If possible, a clean towel or coat should first be placed under the head to prevent injury to the lower eye.

A makeshift twitch

A makeshift twitch can be constructed by passing a loop of soft rope through a hole drilled in the end of a short piece (approx 2–3ft) of broom handle. This can be slipped over the horse's nose and twisted tight, thereby causing the release of endorphins, which will quieten the horse and so help restraint.

■ A makeshift twitch can be used to help restrain a horse.

What do I do if my horse can't get up?

There are a number of reasons why a horse may be recumbent (unable to rise), ranging from simply being physically stuck – for example, in a ditch – to having a severe fracture (Fractures p137), neurological disease (Neurological disease p140), anaphylaxis (Allergies p81), heart (Heart disease p93) or perhaps breathing problems (Respiratory disease p96), or even being winded. In all such cases it is important to get prompt veterinary attention, and while you are waiting for the vet it is usually best to try and keep the horse as quiet as possible and to prevent it struggling, if possible. If safe to do so, try placing a protective pad (for instance, a coat) under the lower eye, and then apply pressure to the back of the horse's head or its upper neck by sitting or kneeling with your weight on this area as this can keep an injured horse down (Restraint p59). However, if a horse is at risk of further injury or drowning, or is having difficulty breathing where it is lying, then attempts can be made to move it, although this can be dangerous.

Blindfolding a conscious horse during such a process can be helpful, although some horses will panic more if blindfolded. Unconscious horses can be moved by the use of brisket and breech ropes (see below), or with well padded ropes around the pasterns, although both methods could be dangerous, particularly if consciousness is regained.

Sometimes pulling the horse right over on to its other side will result in it managing to get to its feet: if it is lying on its near side, loop a soft rope round the near fore and the near hind (preferably – though you can pull on the off-side legs if you can't get to the others), and by pulling on these, roll it on to its off side. Attempts to stand can be helped by a handler at the head and another at the tail, both helping the horse to balance.

know-how: *Moving a recumbent horse*

An unconscious horse can have soft ropes or straps slid underneath it (it may need to be rolled to allow this) and applied to the brisket, breech area and withers (see *right*). Together with a strong buckled headcollar and lead rope this can allow traction to be applied to move a horse whilst keeping control of the head. Padding should be placed under ropes, the cheek straps and behind the ears to prevent nerve damage and chaffing. If possible the horse should be moved onto a tarpaulin or rug that can be used as a stretcher or drag mat.

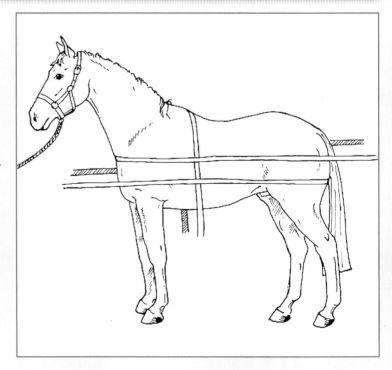

How does choke manifest itself?
What should I do if my horse chokes?

The first sign of choke – or oesophageal obstruction (Choke p104) – is usually that a horse makes repeated unsuccessful attempts to swallow, often stretching out its neck in the process. Dribbling, nasal discharge of food and saliva, distress, heavy breathing and sweating are also often seen, although some horses remain calm and will continue to attempt to eat despite having such an obstruction.

When choke occurs, it is important to call the vet immediately as, although most chokes clear rapidly on their own (usually by the time the vet arrives!), some do not and require emergency medical treatment, the passage of a stomach tube, or even surgery. In addition, pneumonia can follow episodes of choke if food is inhaled. While waiting for the vet, obviously withdraw all food. Little else can be done other than to keep the horse as quiet as possible, though massaging the underside of its neck may be helpful.

■ An oesophageal obstruction or choke can be cleared by passing a stomach tube via the nose.

What are the signs of severe colic?
How quickly should I call a vet?

Colic (Colic p102) simply means abdominal pain, and the signs of this include rolling, flank watching, biting at the flanks, kicking out, sweating, distress and collapse. Loss of appetite and decreased production of dung may also be noted. Some horses with colic, particularly those that have had it for some time, show only mild symptoms of pain such as depression or dullness. An examination of an affected horse by the owner (Making a thorough examination p57–8) may reveal elevated heart and breathing rates (a pulse rate above 60 beats/minute is a particularly bad sign), increased or decreased gut sounds, and the gums may appear a purplish or greyish colour with an increased capillary refill time (Making a thorough examination p57–8) due to circulatory dysfunction. Some horses in pain also have a high rectal temperature.

Colic can occur for a whole range of reasons, varying from constipation to twisting or blockage of the intestines, and the initial symptoms can often be the same, independent of the severity of the underlying condition. In severe cases, irreversible damage to the bowel can occur within about four hours, which can necessitate surgical treatment or euthanasia. This means that colic should always be treated as an emergency situation, and the vet should be called immediately.

Is there anything that can be done while waiting for the vet to arrive?
While awaiting the vet there is little that can be done. Walking horses round may help to take their mind off the pain and stop them rolling but can be dangerous.

to roll it can cause a twist in the gut to develop. In fact there is no evidence of this: twists in the intestines tend to occur due to abnormal movements of the bowel, not because the horse rolls, and though walking some horses may help them to settle, for others it is distressing, if not dangerous. So in fact there is very little that can be done while the vet is awaited, other than withdrawing food and trying to keep an affected horse as quiet as possible.

■ Horses with colic may simply look uncomfortable, or they may show more obvious signs of

How can I stop uncontrolled bleeding?

Any bleeding can be extremely distressing for both horse and owner, but it is important to remember that bleeding usually appears to be very much worse than it is. An average adult horse has around 40 litres (8.8gal) of blood, and so can lose one or two litres (two to four pints) with few ill effects.

Staunching the blood flow can usually be achieved by applying sufficient pressure. A bleeding limb wound can be pressure bandaged (How to apply a pressure bandage, see right) with more and more layers applied until the blood stops coming through the bandage, whilst any wound that cannot be bandaged due to its position can be treated with the application of pressure by hand using a wad of clean towel or some other such fabric. Once pressure has been applied, try not to remove it until the vet comes to assess the wound. This will give the best chance of staunching the blood loss.

Recognizing the type of bleeding

When bleeding occurs, it is helpful to identify the type of bleeding and to get an idea where it is coming from.

➤ **Arterial bleeding** comes directly from the heart at high pressure; it is characterized by bright red blood that spurts from the wound with each heartbeat, and is by far the most dangerous, as large amounts of blood can be lost; the vet should be called immediately if this scenario is suspected.

➤ **Venous bleeding** tends to involve darker blood that seeps, rather than spurts from the wound, and is generally less dangerous. In either case, however, it can be helpful to stop the blood whilst waiting for the vet to arrive.

know-how: How to apply a pressure bandage

NOTE: This is an emergency aid to prevent blood loss. A pressure bandage should not be left on for more than a few hours, or it may cause damage by preventing circulation to the area.

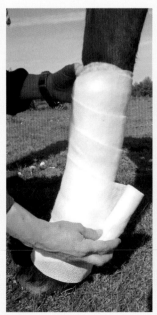

1: Apply a sterile non-adherent dressing to the wound.

2: Hold it in place with an elasticated gauze bandage.

3: Apply a layer of soft conforming bandage, taking it down to cover the coronary band.

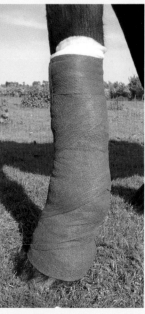

4: Apply pressure with a tightly applied elastic gauze bandage; try to use a figure-of-eight pattern to stop slippage.

5: Repeat steps **3**…

6: …and **4** until no more blood seeps through the bandage.

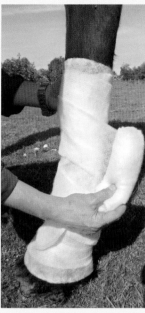

7: Then apply a final tight layer of self-adhesive bandage.

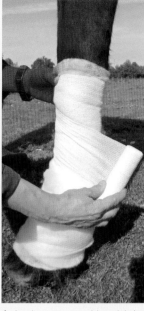

8: The finished bandage should be tight.

What can I do to treat wounds while I wait for the vet?

Firstly, it is important to make an accurate assessment of the severity of the wound(s) and to decide whether an emergency call to the vet is necessary, or whether it can be treated without veterinary advice. Secondly, prompt cleaning of wounds is helpful as, when done properly, this can help to minimize bacterial contamination and maximize the horse's potential to heal the wound without any undue complications. Once cleaned, wounds should be covered to prevent further contamination.

The severity of a wound is dependent on its position, depth and also the degree of contamination, because synovial infections, bone damage or infection and blood loss are all potentially life-threatening.

Being able to make this sort of assessment requires a good working knowledge of your horse's anatomy, in particular the location of his joints and tendons (see page 129) so that careful assessment can be made. Shallow wounds that do not appear to need emergency treatment may be cleaned and dressed initially by the horse's handler. However, most wounds require veterinary attention and medical treatment within 24 hours to prevent or treat infection, and even those horses that have had tetanus innoculations (see Vaccination page 19) may benefit from an extra anti-tetanus injection.

The cleaning of wounds should be carried out with a dilute antiseptic solution; however, it is important to use the right dilution

Wounds requiring emergency treatment

➤ those in the vicinity of joints, tendons, or other synovial structures;
➤ that involve the feet;
➤ that are bleeding heavily;
➤ are associated with obvious bony damage;
➤ are dirty;
➤ are sufficiently large that stitching is required;
➤ that occur on horses that have not been vaccinated regularly against tetanus.

know-how: *Bandaging a wound*

1: Apply a sterile dressing to the wound.

2: Bandage it in place with elasticated net bandage: try to use a figure-of-eight pattern to stop slippage.

3: Apply soft conforming bandage over the injured area and any associated tendons or joints to prevent pressure sores. Cover with a layer of elasticated net bandage to hold firmly in place.

4: Finish with a layer of self-adhesive bandage to keep the dressing clean and dry.

A wound to the fetlock which is one of the danger sites. Wounds near joints are potentially crippling.

of antiseptic at the right pressure, or further cell damage and infection can be caused. The most effective method for cleaning bacteria and debris out of wounds, is to use either a clean syringe or a clean pump-up garden sprayer to wash the wound with antiseptic; otherwise clean cotton wool dipped in antiseptic can be used to wipe the affected area clean.

Ideally all wounds should be cleaned in this way as promptly as possible after they occur. The exception are wounds that are bleeding fast: in these cases the wound is likely to have been washed fairly clean by the blood anyway, and the main priority is to stop the bleeding, rather than worry about cleaning the area. In such cases a sterile dressing should first be applied under a pressure bandage that will stop the bleeding (see How to apply a pressure bandage page 163)

Making up an appropriate antiseptic solution

➤ An appropriate antiseptic solution can be obtained by diluting Betadine® (povidone iodine) 1:8 with water, or Hibiscrub (chlorhexidine) 1:40 with water. Too strong a solution can cause cell damage and delay healing; too weak, and it can fail to reduce bacterial contamination.

pending the vet's arrival.

If there is no heavy, excessive bleeding, time should be taken to clean a wound thoroughly before applying a sterile dressing in order to prevent contamination. After, depending on the injury, bandages should be changed every one to five days, according to the vet's advice.

Wounds that are not fresh also benefit from thorough cleaning and then bandaging. Poulticing (see below) of old and infected wounds is also advisable, and of solar injuries to assist drainage of pus. Medical treatment can be used (see How to give medication page 70) to prevent or control infections and assist healing. Where healing is complicated and proud flesh develops, or excessive scarring occurs (see Wounds page 64), more protracted treatment may be necessary. However, prompt appropriate treatment always gives the best chance of a speedy and full recovery.

know-how: Applying a poultice

5: The finished bandage should be firm but not too tight – you should be able to slide two fingers beneath it.

1: For a wet poultice (generally most useful), first soak the poultice pad in warm water, then apply to the wound.

2: Hold in place with elastic net bandage, using a figure-of-eight pattern to prevent slippage, depending on the wound's position.

3: Cover with a layer of self-adhesive bandage to keep the dressing clean.

4: The finished bandage should be firmly applied.

5: Where possible cover in a layer of plastic, or a boot to keep clean and maintain moisture. Change once or twice daily.

How do I assess swellings? How serious can they be?

A whole range of different causes and types of swelling can occur, ranging from filling of limbs due to cellulitis or lymphangitis, to swellings under the chest and down the limbs due to heart or circulatory failure (Heart disease p93). Swellings can also follow insect and snake bites, allergic reactions (Allergies p81), infection, bruising and cyst formation.

Although limb swellings may appear innocuous, they should always be investigated as they can indicate a serious underlying problem such as an injury, or a heart or circulatory condition. Similarly, unexplained swellings under the tummy and chest should be checked out promptly. Elsewhere on the body, swellings that may be associated with allergies, bites or stings may not be serious in themselves, but they may indicate a serious problem, or may cause difficulty breathing or eating and so may need to be seen promptly. Symptomatic treatment for swelling includes cold hosing of the affected area, and gentle walking.

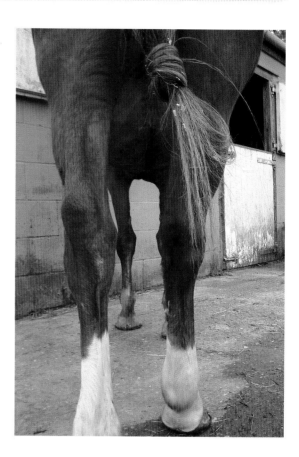

■ Swelling of this horse's right hind limb has resulted in a loss of definition of the tendons and ligaments and in thickening of the limb, which is apparent when the affected limb is compared with the left hind limb.

What can I do to help my horse if he has difficulty breathing?

Difficulty breathing is always an emergency situation that necessitates immediate veterinary attention. It can result from chest or neck injuries, or infections, or it can be a rapid consequence of allergic reactions (Allergies p81) – but whatever the cause, there is little that can be done to help affected horses while awaiting the vet other than providing a quiet, calm environment that will help to reduce stress and prevent panicking. Where possible, food and other material may be removed from the mouth in order to clear the airway, and if an affected horse is down, extending the head and neck may be helpful.

In an emergency situation, a vet may need to pass a tube into the lungs, alternatively he may perform a tracheostomy (cut an opening in the windpipe in the neck) for the horse to breathe through. Emergency medication may also be necessary. Horses with breathing problems have the best chance of survival if they receive prompt veterinary attention.

How can I tell if my horse is lame? What should I do if he is?

It can be really hard to tell whether or not a horse is lame (Lameness p119), and the basic rule is, if in doubt – ask the vet! Obviously severe acute (sudden) lamenesses are usually manifested by obvious hobbling, head nodding, or an uneven sensation as the horse moves under saddle. However, more subtle lamenesses, or those that come on gradually, may be harder to detect and may only be manifested as difficulty working on a circle, inability to work on both diagonals at trot, or both leads at canter, moving disunited at canter, or even simply loss of performance and refusals.

Once you have identified the lame limb, it can be helpful to have a feel of all the limbs, looking out for any areas of heat, pain, swelling or lack of flexibility. This may help you to identify the source of the lameness, and provide you with information that will be helpful to the vet. Lame horses should be box rested in order to prevent further injury, pending a veterinary diagnosis. In the meantime, cold hosing or the use of cold boots may help to reduce inflammation in areas of warmth or swelling, and a support bandage can be applied (How to apply a support bandage p68). This is used to support the injured limb when tendon injury is known or suspected, or to support the tendons of the opposite sound limb in cases of severe lameness, as it will be bearing comparatively more weight.

> ### How lameness is graded
>
> Lameness is normally graded on a scale of 1–10 to aid objectivity:
> - ➤ **Grade 0:** Sound.
> - ➤ **Grade 2/10:** Lameness hard to detect at walk or trot.
> - ➤ **Grade 4/10:** Lameness barely detectable at walk, easy to see at trot.
> - ➤ **Grade 6/10:** Easily detectable lameness at walk.
> - ➤ **Grade 8/10:** Hobbling at walk. Unable/unwilling to trot.
> - ➤ **Grade 10/10:** Non weight-bearing.

know-how: *Performing a lameness examination*

The best way to assess a horse that you think may be lame is to ask a friend to walk and trot it up in hand in a straight line on a hard, firm surface for around 20 yards (18m) on a loose rein.

- As the horse goes away from you, watch the pelvis and try to see if it is moving symmetrically. Also watch the hocks and hooves, and try and check that they are moving the same amount as each other.
- As it returns towards you, watch the head carefully and try to see if there is a consistent head nod, and whether the forelimbs are moving symmetrically.
- Also watch the horse go past you, or trot it up in raked sand, and try and check that the stride lengths are symmetrical and that it is tracking up properly.
- Trotting a shod horse on the road can also be helpful, as the lame foot generally makes a quieter sound on the tarmac as it bears less weight.
- Working the horse on a circle can also aid lameness detection – this normally exacerbates lameness when the affected limb is on the inside of the circle and thus bearing comparatively more weight. This exercise can be particularly helpful if a horse is lame bilaterally, as it may be hard to see overt lameness in a straight line – the horse may merely appear 'pottery'. On a circle, however, the inside leg on either rein usually appears the lamest.
- Hindlimb lamenesses tend to be manifested as 'dropping of the hip' on the sound leg as it bears weight, while the lame leg tenses up as it bears weight.
- Forelimb lamenesses are generally easier to assess as normally the head nods up as the lame leg bears weight.

- Severe lameness (left) is manifested by obvious hobbling and nodding of the head. More subtle lameness (right) is best appreciated by watching the horse being led up on a firm flat surface.

What can I do for a horse that can't bear weight on a leg?

Non-weight-bearing lameness is always an emergency situation because the causes of lameness this profound include fractures (Fractures p137), severe tendon injuries (Tendon injuries p128), joint infections (Joint infections p136) and nerve damage, all of which need prompt treatment for the best chance of recovery. While awaiting the vet, try not to move or walk the horse. If the horse is distressed, attempts should be made to restrain it (Restraint p59) in order to prevent further injury, as long as it is safe to do this. It may be helpful to keep recumbent horses down by applying pressure to the head/neck (Recumbency p60), and standing horses may be restrained using a twitch or rope. If an injured horse must be moved, use a horse-box or trailer. Examination of the injured limb, or treatment of anything other than bleeding wounds, is not recommended as this may cause further pain and distress. If a fracture is known or suspected to be present, a support bandage or a splint (How to apply a limb support bandage or splint, below) may be used to assist pain relief during transport to a place where further treatment can be carried out, but application of this type of bandage is best left to the vet, because if it is applied incorrectly, such a bandage can do more harm than good. A tendon support bandage (How to apply a tendon support bandage, p69) may be used to try to support the affected limb if a tendon injury is suspected, or to support the other limbs when they are bearing more weight because the horse is not bearing weight on the injured limb.

Prompt veterinary assessment and treatment is of paramount importance to the welfare of such horses.

know-how: *The limb support bandage*

A support bandage can be used to provide stability to an area of the limb if a fracture, or a severe tendon or ligament injury, is suspected.

Like a pressure bandage (How to apply a pressure bandage p63), a support bandage (*right*) is achieved by repeating alternating layers of soft padding bandages with elastic bandages applied fairly tightly. Normally at least three pairs of layers are used so that the bandage provides sufficient support that the horse cannot move the joints within the bandage. To provide sufficient stability it is normally necessary to incorporate at least one normal joint on either side of the injury (for instance, if the injury is suspected to be in the fetlock area, make sure the bandage goes above the knee or the hock).

Further stability can be achieved by incorporating a firm splint, such as a piece of wood, into the bandage to hold the affected area straight (as long as the splint is sufficiently strong not to break, and sufficiently well padded so as not to cause further injury). Such a bandage cannot be left on long or it can cause circulatory problems, but it can be a helpful temporary measure to allow transfer of an injured horse to a hospital for further assessment and treatment.

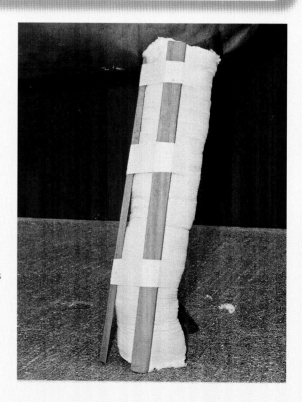

■ Injuries incurred during strenuous activity can be very serious. Any suspected tendon injury should be attended to promptly.

know-how: *The tendon bandage*

If a tendon injury is suspected, it is important to bandage the affected limb to provide support.

1: Wrap a foam or gamgee pad, or a thick layer of cotton wool around the lower limb.

2: Using an elastic net bandage or tail bandage, bandage firmly from the knee or hock to the fetlock, leaving the pad showing at both ends to avoid putting excessive pressure on the skin.

3: The finished bandage should be firm but not too tight: it should be possible to slide two fingers beneath it. Such a bandage should be changed at least twice daily to avoid pressure sores.

How do you take off a shoe in an emergency?

There are a number of reasons why it may be necessary to remove a shoe. Sometimes it comes partly off and a horse then treads on it, or is at risk of doing so (Solar punctures p121). Alternatively the shoe may be suspected of causing lameness (for instance in 'nail bind', when lameness develops rapidly following farriery due to one of the nails being too close to the white line, which contains the sensitive laminae). Although your farrier should view such problems as emergencies and be happy to come promptly and remove a horse's shoe himself, valuable time can be saved and further injuries prevented by immediate removal of problem shoes.

You can really only take off a shoe with a shoe-removing kit; it should include a hammer, a wedge-shaped 'buffer', and nail removers.

Before attempting to remove a shoe ensure that the horse is adequately restrained and that you can hold up and support his foot between your knees. Bear in mind that if the foot is painful, the horse may resent attempts to remove the shoe, and sedation or nerve blocking of the foot may be necessary. If in any doubt about what to do, call a vet or farrier.

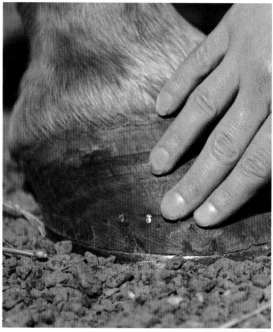

■ Check clenches regularly to reduce the chance of an unexpected lost shoe.

know-how: Removing a shoe

1: With the foot upturned, slide the wedge of the buffer under the clenches and hammer them all up. Alternatively a rasp may be used to rasp off the clenches.

2: Grasp each nail in turn from the underside of the shoe using the nail pullers, and remove it (and don't then leave them lying around where they can be trodden on).

3: As soon as the shoe is sufficiently loose it can be levered up and lifted off.

4: The foot should then be examined carefully for any signs of injuries such as punctures of the sole. If any are found, or if the horse's lameness persists, prompt veterinary attention should be sought. In the meantime it may be helpful to poultice the foot (see Applying a poultice p65).

What are the basic classes of medication used for horses?

Amongst the medicines used for horses, antibiotics and anti-inflammatories are by far the most common.

Antibiotics

➤ Work by killing bacteria, or preventing them from breeding so that the horse's natural resistance to infection can eliminate them.

➤ Some penetrate areas of the body better than others, so the choice of which to use depends on the type of infection and the practicalities of administering medicines.

➤ Normally few side effects, but long courses of antibiotics can disrupt intestinal bacteria and cause diarrhoea, so using probiotics is often advisable.

➤ Ensure that the right dose is given at the correct interval, and finish the course. Incorrect use can restrict effectiveness, and result in the development of bacteria that are resistant to the antibiotic.

Anti-inflammatories

➤ Most commonly used types are non-steroidal anti-inflammatory drugs (known as NSAIDS). These include bute (phenylbutazone).

➤ Reduce pain, high temperatures and inflammation, and can be used in the long or short term to treat conditions like low grade lameness (Lameness p119).

➤ Usually the dose can be gradually reduced to the lowest that is effective, or they can be used on an 'as and when' basis for an intermittent problem.

What medicines are safe to keep in the tack box for home use?

➤ No medicines should ever be used without the advice of a veterinary surgeon.

➤ Any medicines should be kept in a locked box, and only used for the horse for which they were prescribed, or for another on the advice of a vet.

➤ Courses of medication should always be finished or they are likely to be ineffective.

➤ Any left-over medicines, or medicines that become out of date (always check the expiry date), together with any packaging, bottles, syringes and needles, should be returned to the vet for disposal.

Applying topical medicines

➤ Ensure that the horse is adequately restrained.

➤ Apply topical medication wearing gloves if necessary and following the instructions of the vet.

➤ **To apply medication to the eye:** use one hand to part the eyelids, and the other to apply the medication to the surface of the eye or the inside of the bottom eyelid. Ensure that the nozzle of the tube does not touch the eye. Allow the eye to close: the horse's natural blinking action will disperse the medication.

➤ They are usually very safe, but occasionally they can cause severe diarrhoea, or, particularly at high doses in the long term, can be associated with a range of problems including liver or kidney disease.

➤ Side effects should be reported to the vet promptly, and the medicine stopped in the meantime. Regular monitoring of horses is also important if they are being used in the long term.

Steroids are useful for treating problems such as allergic conditions (Allergies p81), but do carry the risk of inducing laminitis (Laminitis p122) and so should be used at the lowest possible dose, particularly in laminitis-prone ponies.

Other medicines include hormonal treatments, sedatives, and medicines for Cushing's disease (Cushing's disease p143). Food supplements and nutraceuticals (food supplements with medicinal qualities) may be used in certain circumstances, for example, glucosamine for chronic arthritis (Arthritis p135). All horses should be monitored carefully, and any problems investigated by the prescribing vet.

How do I give oral medications and injections?

Some medicines can only be given by injection, while others only work orally. Yet others can be given by either route, and a choice must be made in each individual case as to the most appropriate method. The benefits of injecting include the fact that the medicines get into the body system more quickly, but oral administration is usually preferable because most horses resent it less than being regularly injected.

Whilst many horses will take oral medicines if they are simply mixed in feed, some refuse to do so. For these there are various techniques that can be used. Medicines can, of course, be put into food that is particularly tasty, and a little molasses, garlic, peppermint cordial or sugar-beet water can sometimes hide the taste of medicines. Where this does not work, it can be helpful to core out an apple or a carrot and hide the medication within, or, in the

worst cases, an old, clean worming syringe can be used to give the medicine (mixed up with water or molasses as appropriate) directly into the mouth. If even this doesn't work, there may be an argument for using injectable medicines in such horses.

Although vets can give medicines into the vein and directly into joints as well as into the muscle, the only practicable route for owners to use at home is the intramuscular one. This can be used in horses that refuse to take oral medicines, or those that require medicines that are only available as injections that can be given intramuscularly. Extreme care should be taken in all cases, as there is a risk that owners may be injured in the process, and adequate restraint (Restraint p59) should therefore be used. Should accidental self-injection of any horse medicines occur, it is of paramount importance to seek immediate medical attention.

know-how: *Identify your injection site*

Identify your injection site: there are three main options:

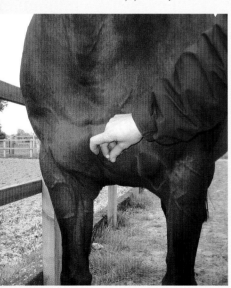  

■ The soft, fleshy muscle on either side of the brisket.

■ The neck muscle, half way between the mane and the underside of the neck and a hand's breadth in front of the front of the shoulder.

■ The muscle of the rump midway between the point of the hip and the base of the tail.

know-how: How to give an intramuscular injection

NOTE: Injections should only be given on the advice of the vet. Return used needles and sharps to your vet to dispose of. If you are unsure or unhappy about any stage in this process do not proceed, but first discuss matters further with your vet.

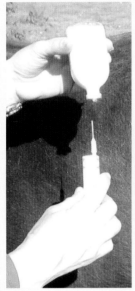 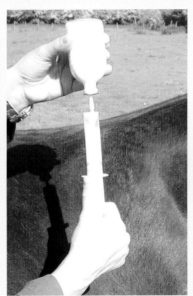 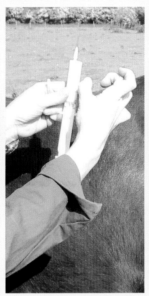 

1: Ensure the horse is adequately restrained. Shake the medicine bottle well.

2: Draw up the dose of medicine into a sterile syringe using a sterile needle, having first swabbed the top of the medicine bottle with surgical spirit to prevent contamination of the needle. It may help to inject the same volume of air into the bottle first, as you intend to withdraw of medicine.

3: Ensure there are no air bubbles: holding the syringe upright and flicking it can help them to rise to the needle so they can be expressed. Replace the needle cap on the needle.

4: Identify your injection site (see *know-how*, opposite). Remove needle, and with a firm, confident motion pat the area once or twice and then insert the needle firmly right up to the hub.

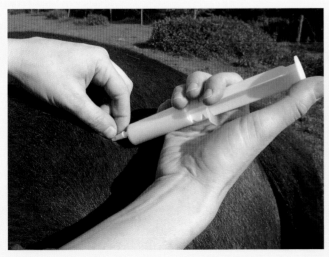 

5: Hook on the syringe and draw back on the plunger. If blood enters the hub of the syringe, remove it and insert a new needle in a different place – some intramuscular medicines can be extremely dangerous if inadvertently injected into a blood vessel.

6: If no blood is seen, depress the plunger firmly to inject the medicine. If you encounter resistance, stop, remove the needle, and try again in a new position. On completion, remove the needle and rub the area to disperse the medication and relieve discomfort.

What are the options for euthanasia and disposal of a horse's body?

None of us likes to consider the fact that euthanasia of our horses may become necessary; however, there are some injuries and conditions which just aren't treatable, and for which euthanasia is the only option. These include horses with untreatable fractures, synovial (joint and tendon sheath) infections, some types of neurological (nerve-related) disease, and any condition that causes unremitting pain or suffering. It may also be necessary to consider euthanasia when treating severe conditions if sufficient funds are not available for appropriate treatment, rather than subject a horse to treatment with little or no chance of success, and thus further suffering. Permission for euthanasia should be sought from insurance companies for those horses that are insured, unless the horse is in constant and unremitting pain and immediate euthanasia on humane grounds is necessary.

There are basically two main methods of euthanasia: either with a gun, or by lethal injection. The choice of technique may be based on whichever method is available to alleviate the horse's pain and suffering the fastest, or which method is most appropriate for a horse depending on the type of disease it has. Those horses that are difficult to handle may first need to be sedated.

A gun can be used by a vet or licensed horse slaughterer, and results in immediate loss of consciousness and death, although the noise and subsequent reflex activity may make this method more upsetting for the owners. A lethal injection can only be administered by a vet, and whilst a little more preparation time is needed (a catheter usually has to be put into the vein first), and the response to the injection also takes a little time, some owners find this less upsetting.

DISPOSING OF THE BODY

There are three main methods for disposal of the horse's body. Horses that are euthanased using a gun may enter the human or animal food chain if they are euthanased in an abbatoir. If euthanased by this method at home, horse slaughterers and huntsmen may use a horse's carcass for various purposes, or alternatively burial or cremation may be options. If a lethal injection has been used, burial and cremation are the only appropriate methods of carcase disposal. However, recent legislation means that burial is not always allowed, though it may be possible in certain areas, given permission from the local council or environmental authority. Cremation in a pet crematorium is probably the most commonly used means of disposal of horses' bodies these days, although it is relatively expensive. Local vets can put owners in contact with nearby huntsmen, horse slaughterers and pet crematoria.

Skin disease

The head

Diseases of the heart and circulation

Respiratory conditions

5: Common diseases

What causes skin diseases in horses?

There are many potential causes of skin disease in horses, ranging from poor diet (Feeding p24) to parasites, allergies (Allergies p81) to tumours (Tumours p83) and injuries (Wounds p64, 85) to infections. The visible symptoms include hair loss and scurfy skin, as well as lumps, bumps, injuries and swellings.

Horses that have had a poor start in life commonly have scurfy skin and a dull coat, and this is often due to a combination of an inadequate diet (Feeding p24) and parasites such as lice and chorioptic mange. Such a horse is therefore bound to benefit from a gradual improvement in diet, and control of any parasites. Lice are 1–3mm long, and can generally be found clinging to hairs, often most obviously in or under the mane. Mange mites are smaller and cannot be seen without a microscope, so a veterinary examination may therefore be called for, and anti-parasitic treatment may be needed.

Older horses on a good diet that have had no contact with

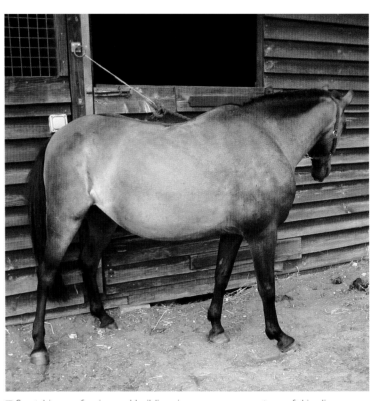

■ Scratching on fencing and buildings is a common symptom of skin disease.

parasites tend to be less likely to get any skin problems, though injuries and tumours can affect any individual. Any signs of a problem should be investigated promptly by a vet, and in addition

to medication, a food balancer or vitamin/ mineral supplement may improve the quality of the skin and coat in horses that are fed on a predominantly forage diet (Feeding p24).

■ Adult and larval lice (up to 2–3mm long) may be found on the coat, causing itchiness and sometimes blood loss.

■ Ticks (around 5mm long) are a common problem in parts of the country where horses are kept near sheep or deer.

■ Harvest mites (that cannot be seen with the naked eye) can also cause severe itchiness of the lower limbs, as can chorioptes mites.

My cob is always scratching his legs: what can I do?

A number of factors can cause horses to scratch their legs. Typical behaviour includes biting and chewing at their limbs, scratching one limb against another or on fencing, and stamping and kicking out for no apparent reason. Symptoms like this can be part of a behavioural syndrome of self-injury due to boredom, but are more often associated with skin disease of the limbs. Mud fever may be involved (Mud fever p80), and chorioptes mange infestation is also a common problem, particularly in cobby breeds with a great deal of feather. Other factors include skin infection, the itchiness of healing wounds or injuries, irritation caused by other biting insects such as ticks and harvest mites, and sensitivity due to abrasive dirt and moisture held in the coat.

TREATMENT

The most effective way to deal with horses that consistently suffer from lower limb irritation is to:

➤ Clip out the limbs and keep them clipped short; this in itself helps to keep the skin clean and dry.

➤ Regular shampooing with an antiseptic shampoo such as Hibiscrub (chlorhexidine) or Betadine (povidone iodine) is also helpful (Using antiseptic p65).

➤ In addition, veterinary examination and possibly lab tests might indicate the use of anti-parasitic sprays or shampoos to treat external parasites, and antibiotics to treat infection.

■ Cobs with heavy feather are particularly prone to itchiness of the limbs.

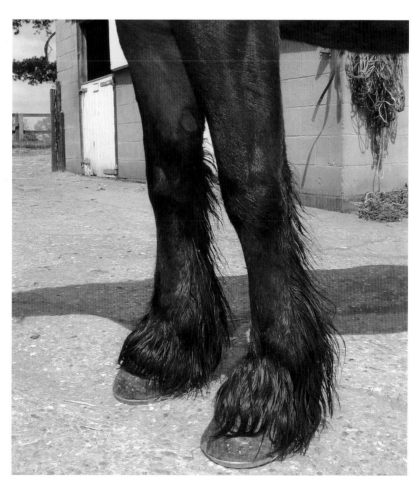

What causes mud fever and what can I do to control it?

Both mud fever and rain scald are caused by a bacterium called *Dermatophilus congolensis*, which is commonly found in the soil and on the skin. The bacteria only causes problems if it gains access to softened or damaged skin, and then it can cause dermatitis (skin inflammation) with symptoms including reddening of the skin, crustiness, itchiness, irritation and hair loss. This is most commonly seen as mud fever in horses on muddy fields whose skin around the heels and pasterns is constantly wet and dirty, or as rain scald on the body in the run-off areas where wet weather keeps the skin and coat moist. Both tend to be worse on any skin that is unpigmented, as this seems to be weaker. Mild sunburn may also be a predisposing factor (Sunburn p45), as may any other cause of skin damage. In affected areas, patches of hair lift off the infected skin attached to the crusty exudate caused by the infection: these resemble a paint brush – called the 'paint brush' lesion, and typical of this disease – leaving reddened, swollen skin beneath.

■ Unsightly and sore, rain scald is caused by bacteria.

TREATMENT

Treatment includes:

➤ Trimming the hair over affected areas, and washing daily with antiseptic solution such as Hibiscrub or Betadine.

➤ Affected areas should then be dried with a clean paper towel, and a barrier cream applied to prevent access of moisture, dirt and further bacteria.

➤ Antibiotics are also needed in many cases – although creams containing corticosteroids should generally be avoided, as they can very often exacerbate the condition.

To prevent the condition:

➤ Try to keep susceptible horses clean and dry and out of mud.

➤ Avoid predisposing factors such as sunburn, photosensitivity, tick bites and overreaching, particularly in warm, wet weather.

➤ Clipping, cleaning, and use of such a barrier cream is also highly effective as a preventative measure against mud fever.

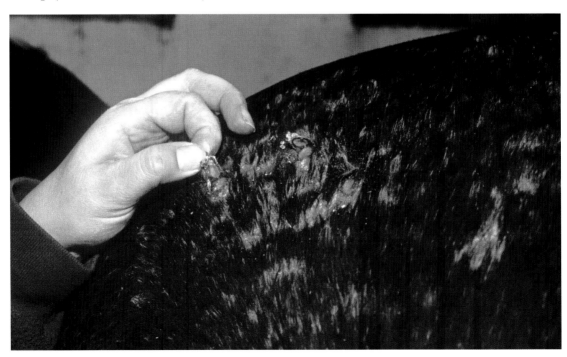

My mare got urticaria once: why? What can I do if it happens again?

In around 50 per cent of cases where a horse develops urticaria (a nettle rash or hives, which usually indicates an allergic reaction) the cause is never found, and most of these cases respond promptly to treatment and never recur. However, urticaria is only one of the symptoms of an allergic reaction, and in some cases other symptoms develop, such as diarrhoea (Diarrhoea p105) or breathing difficulties (Respiratory disease p96) due to swelling of the throat and settling of fluid in the lungs. Such symptoms can occasionally be rapidly fatal if not treated promptly, so it is always advisable to seek prompt veterinary attention for any cases of urticaria, and to try to identify the cause, so that, if possible, it can be avoided in the future.

Typically, swellings come up over the horse's skin, which look almost like bubble wrap and may be sensitive to the touch or itchy. They can come up within a matter of minutes, or develop more slowly over several days, and whilst they are often initially seen over the neck and trunk, they can affect the whole body.

Common causes include skin contact with an allergen – for example the washing powder used on rugs, or clipper oil, or certain grooming products – or a dietary ingredient to which the horse is allergic (Feeding p24), or the inhalation of an allergen (for instance, certain pollens: Respiratory disease p96). A range of other items can be involved, from recent infections, to medicines, snake bites and stinging-nettle stings.

What is allergy testing?

A horse's sensitivity to various allergens can be evaluated using either blood allergy testing (which tests for certain antibodies in the blood) or skin-patch testing (which involves injecting tiny quantities of various potential allergens, and seeing which elicit an allergic response). This can be extremely helpful in allowing owners to exclude potential allergens and thus reduce the likelihood of skin or respiratory allergies. It can also be used in the development of immunotherapy medicines, which can be used to reduce a horse's sensitivity to specific allergens.

TREATMENT

➤ Prompt treatment with corticosteroids is usually effective, although other medicines may also be used.

➤ Future avoidance of the allergen is obviously advisable, although this can be quite difficult if it was not identified.

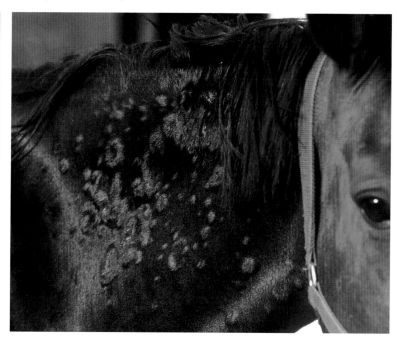

■ Urticaria, or hives, causes swellings to form within the skin, and is usually associated with an allergic response.

I'm thinking about buying a horse with sarcoids. Is this wise?

Sarcoids are skin masses that, although thought to be induced by a virus, behave like tumours and can result in horses becoming unridable due to irritation caused by tack or flies. Although some sarcoids cause few problems and are merely unsightly, others cause extensive areas of ulceration and associated pain, and can become severe enough to necessitate euthanasia.

Several different types of sarcoid can develop, ranging from flaky 'occult' lesions on the skin, to warty 'verrucose' lumps, or large pedunculated and ulcerated masses. One of the major problems with this condition is that treatment is not always successful (success rates are around 80 per cent, at best), and in some cases sarcoids get worse, rather than better, following biopsy sampling or treatment. This means that those sarcoids (or

◼ Other masses, such as papillomas on this young horse's muzzle, can resemble sarcoids.

suspected sarcoids) that are not causing clinical problems at any particular time may be best left untreated until they do.

If considering purchasing a horse with pre-existing sarcoids (see Pre-purchase examinations page 8), it is important to bear in

mind that the condition can be potentially disabling and very expensive to treat, and that the horse would be uninsurable for any fees relating to this condition. While people do buy horses with pre-existing sarcoids, they would really have to be exceptional animals for this to be worthwhile.

TREATMENT

Treatment options include:

➤ surgical removal
➤ radiation therapy
➤ cryotherapy
➤ lasertherapy
➤ immunotherapy
➤ chemotherapy (see Glossary page 149)

Furthermore all treatments are expensive, with horses often requiring ongoing or repeated treatments.

◼ Ulcerated verrucose sarcoid adjacent to the elbow.

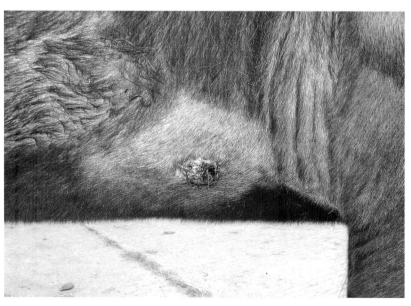

What causes the skin lumps on my horse's back?

Skin lumps on a horse's back can occur for a number of reasons. An ill-fitting saddle is a common problem and, quite apart from saddle sores (Tack p22), can result in the development of small, hard lumps of fibrous tissue in the saddle area. Fly bites (Insects p21) and irritation due to midges (Sweet itch p84) are other common problems, and can cause swellings and nodules to develop, as can the aberrant migration of some intestinal parasites.

Finally, a number of types of skin tumour can develop, which may also have a similar appearance. Skin tumours ranging from melanomas (particularly common in grey horses) to squamous cell carcinomas can also appear elsewhere on other parts of the body.

(Tack p22) ... (Insects p21) ... (Sweet itch p84)

TREATMENT

➤ As long as small skin lumps cause few problems, leaving them alone may be an option.

➤ However, lumps that grow rapidly, or that cause pain or sensitivity when touched, may need to be either biopsied or removed, and this treatment may necessitate several weeks off work while the wounds are healing.

➤ Where masses on the back are concerned, it is also important to make sure that tack is a good fit, and that the skin circulation to affected areas is optimized by using a gel pad or foam pad under the saddle to reduce the pressure in the area; massage may also be helpful.

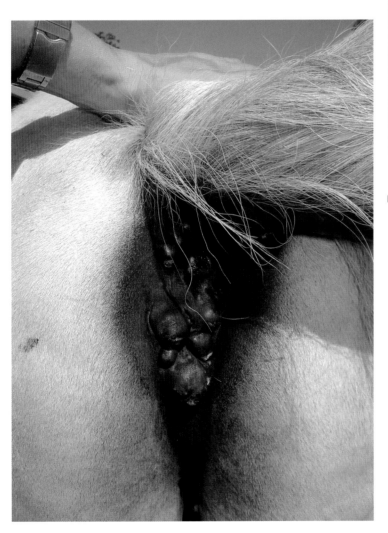

■ Melanomas are particularly common in grey horses, and can occur anywhere on the body. These ones under the horse's dock may interfere with dunging if they enlarge any further.

My pony gets sweet itch. What causes this, and how do I treat it?

Sweet itch is caused by a sensitivity or allergy to the saliva of the Culicoides midge (Insects p21), which results in severe itchiness and skin irritation. Affected horses and ponies usually have characteristic lesions in their mane, along their back, and at their tail base, although most of the midge bites actually occur in the groin area and on the underside of the tummy.

TREATMENT

Keeping out of the way of bites is the best way to avoid this condition, as none of the potential treatments is completely effective. This can be done by:

➤ Stabling at dawn and dusk.

➤ Using effective fly repellents (it is important to remember to apply these to the tummy and groin areas as well as elsewhere, since this is where most of the bites occur).

➤ The use of a fly rug that protects the horse's underside and neck is also advisable, bcause this helps to prevent the mites penetrating right down to the skin. It also helps to protect the horse from damaging itself by scratching.

■ Sweet itch causes severe irritation, itchiness and self-injury, which is particularly marked along the neck and back.

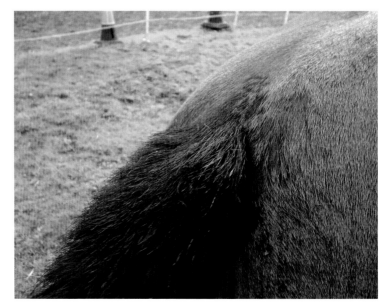

■ The tail base is also commonly affected in ponies with sweet itch.

Can you please tell me more about how to deal with wounds?

The final outcome for a horse or pony that has had a wound is highly dependent not only on the position and severity of the wound itself, but also the rapidity with which it received appropriate first aid (Wounds p64), ongoing treatment and convalescent management. Wounds seen by vets within four hours of their occurrence have a reasonable chance of being stitchable, of then healing rapidly with minimal scarring, and so causing few future problems. However, those horses that are not dealt with appropriately in the first instance have a much higher chance of developing complications such as wound infection and breakdown of the sutures, which at best may lead to a much longer period of convalescence, and at worst can lead to severe problems such as are associated with scarring, as well as tetanus and potentially fatal infections.

Other complications that can prove fatal include infection of synovial structures (joints and tendons). Whilst intensive early treatment involving flushing the affected area with antiseptics and

Signs of tetanus

➤ Progressive muscle spasm and paralysis, which generally prove fatal.
➤ One of the first obvious signs is that the third eyelid (the membrane in the corner of the eyes) becomes visible.
➤ Other signs include spasm of all the body muscles leading to difficulty breathing, and a stance like a 'saw horse'.

If any such symptoms are suspected, prompt and aggressive medical therapy is absolutely essential if the affected horse is to have any chance of survival.

TREATMENT

The principles of wound management for the best outcome include:

➤ calling the vet out immediately to initiate appropriate treatment;
➤ cleaning the wound as promptly as possible (How to clean a wound p64) with appropriate antiseptic;
➤ ensuring that the vet's advice with regard to rest, wound dressings and medication is followed.

Complications are generally associated with those wounds that:

➤ are not seen promptly;
➤ are not cleaned adequately, and kept clean by regular changes of sterile dressings;
➤ and with those horses that are not sufficiently rested during wound healing,
➤ or that don't receive their full course of medication – often because they won't take it in food (Medication p72).

Anti-tetanus medication is also essential for:

➤ horses with wounds, and even vaccinated horses (Vaccines p19) may benefit from tetanus anti-toxin (a ready-made boost to their tetanus immunity) when wounds are dirty and contaminated with soil;
➤ any unvaccinated horses should receive tetanus anti-toxin as soon as possible after sustaining even the most apparently minor wound.
➤ It is also important that foals are vaccinated promptly after birth, or tetanus could result.

antibiotics can be helpful, treatment with systemic antibiotics is also important. Despite such measures, some horses with even apparently minor wounds die due to uncontrollable infection. Any wounds in the vicinity of joints or tendons and ligaments should therefore be taken seriously and should receive prompt and effective medical treatment.

Wounds that don't get infected may heal by what is called primary intention (that is, along the suture line), and can heal within 10–14 days (although they won't have gained full strength at that stage) and will scar little, if at all.

SECONDARY INTENTION WOUNDS

Wounds that break down due to movement and/ or infection will generally tend to gape open, and then have to heal by what is called secondary intention healing. This involves the tissues around the wound contracting so as to minimize the size of the wound, and then a bed of granulation tissue forms: this is a reddish, rough tissue with a high level of blood circulation that seals the wounds and forms a base for skin to grow across. Skin then grows in from the edges of the lesion to cover the granulation tissue at speeds of up to 2–3mm a day, if no infection is present and as long as the wound is kept immobile. Depending on the size of the wound, this can take weeks to months, and the costs of ongoing bandaging and medicines inevitably add up.

Bandaging, despite its high cost, has an important role to play in the immobilization of the affected area, also in keeping it clean, and in controlling swelling. Secondary intention wounds on mobile areas (for example, close to joints) or that are chronically infected, have a tendency to produce exuberant granulation tissue or proud flesh, which bulges from the wound and slows the skin growth at the wound edges. If left untreated this can contribute to a poor aesthetic appearance of the healed area (large lumps tend to result) and it can also affect future mobility, as well as delaying healing. It is therefore important to treat proud flesh aggressively, usually by cutting it back surgically to enable skin formation to cover the wound.

Once the wound is stable, and the skin has healed or almost healed, it may be possible to start increasing exercise. If this is done gradually this will encourage a better blood supply to any scar tissue (which in turn will help it to become softer and function better) without putting the healed area under undue stress. Massage and laser therapy (Physiotherapy p13) may also help encourage the remodelling of scar tissue to improve its function, which in turn aids mobility and helps prevent mechanical restrictions to movement, which can cause lameness.

Fly strike

Open wounds, ulcerated masses or scalded skin that are associated with chronic discharges are all vulnerable to flies, that can cause irritation and fly strike. Fly strike occurs when blowflies lay their eggs in open skin, and the maggots that hatch out within a few hours start to eat the surrounding flesh. This can cause severe damage to affected areas, as well as infection. In order to prevent fly strike, wounds should be covered (where possible), fly repellents should be used, and wound dressings containing insecticides can also be helpful.

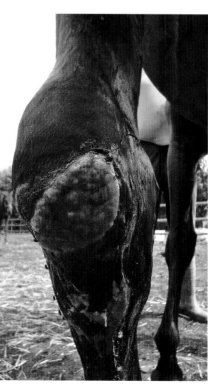
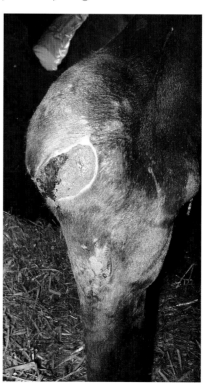

■ Wounds in high motion areas such as this one on the back of a horse's hock are particularly prone to the development of proud flesh. This wound is also infected and attracting flies, which carry a risk of fly strike. Two weeks later this wound is responding well to limb bandaging to reduce movement, to removal of proud flesh, and to antibiotic therapy to treat infection.

What is moon blindness? Is it the same as uveitis?

Moon blindness, recurrent uveitis and periodic opthalmia are all terms used to describe a condition involving severe inflammation within the eye that can occur for a number of reasons, and may crop up again from time to time in the future. Uveitis may follow bacterial or viral infections within the eye, or may be a response to injuries or even tumours.

Whatever may be the cause, this condition is characterized by the affected horse suddenly developing a very painful eye, with symptoms including swelling of the eyelids, blinking in response to light, increased tear production, and reddening of the ocular membranes and the eye itself. In severe cases the front part of the eye can be discoloured by the presence of blood or pus within the front chamber, or obscured by opacity of the front surface of the eye. If not treated promptly and aggressively horses can have ongoing problems with reduced vision in the affected eye due to loss of clarity within the eye. Also, adhesions can develop between different parts of the eye that affect the ability of the pupil to react to light, and damage to the lens and fibrous changes within the eye may also occur.

Even with early treatment some cases of uveitis

TREATMENT

Any symptoms of eye disease should always be seen as soon as possible by a vet, as the more promptly that effective treatment is initiated, the better the chance of a full recovery. Treatment usually includes:

➤ a combination of both topical and systemic medicines including antibiotics, anti-inflammatories and mydriatics (medicines to cause temporary dilation of the pupil to keep it mobile and help reduce pain). It is extremely important to persevere with giving the medicines, even if this is difficult (How to apply eye medication p72).

are recurrent, causing the affected horse to be unable to work during times of disease, and potentially contributing to a gradual reduction in vision in the affected eye. This means that purchase of horses with recurrent uveitis, or signs that indicate that they have had uveitis in the past (and therefore might again), should be considered very carefully (Pre-purchase examinations p8).

■ Uveitis causes severe inflammation of the affected eye, with whitening of the front surface of the eye and excessive tear production.

How significant is blindness in one eye: what can cause blindness?

The potential causes of blindness range from eye injuries, infections and tumours, to uveitis, cataracts and retinal disease. In some cases it is immediately obvious that a horse has a problem that prevents him from being able to see, in others the eye may appear externally normal and yet still have defective or absent vision, making the horse blind on that side. Where defective vision is suspected, a simple check involves feinting a finger at the eye without touching it or the eyelashes, and seeing if the horse blinks (called the menace response). Another is to test if the pupils narrow in response to bright light (called the pupillary light reflex) by shining a bright light at the eye in a darkened stable.

Before buying a horse or even taking one on loan, it is always advisable to have the eyes checked thoroughly as part of a pre-purchase examination (Pre-purchase examinations p8), and any signs of abnormality that are noticed should be investigated further. If blindness exists but affects one eye only, this may not be too much of a problem, depending on the horse's function. However, if both eyes are affected, or are likely to become affected with the same condition, the horse's working life will be reduced, and those horses whose work requires judging of distance (such as jumping) really need to have two functioning eyes.

It is also important to bear in mind that horses that are blind in one eye should always be approached from their seeing side, and should be treated with care. In addition, they often hold their head to one side to maximize their field of view, so they may suffer from neck stiffness and pain, and need regular physiotherapy (Physiotherapy p13).

I think there's a tiny lump in my horse's eye: is this serious?

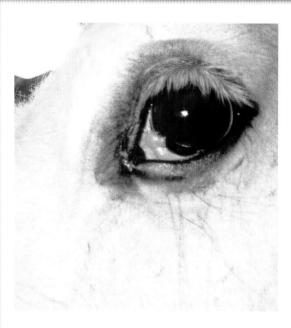

The eyes and their surrounding tissues are one of the areas of the body where tumours sometimes occur, and any lump or bump seen in the proximity of an eye, however tiny, is cause for concern and calls for a prompt check-up from the vet. Sarcoids (Sarcoids p82) can occur close to the eyes, and tumours such as squamous cell carcinomas and melanomas can occur within the eye, or associated with the membranes surrounding the eyes. If they are recognized and removed promptly, such masses may not cause ongoing problems, but in some cases radiotherapy, chemotherapy and even removal of the eye are necessary.

■ The small mass in the corner of this horse's eye was a squamous cell carcinoma that could have proved fatal had it not been identified and removed promptly.

My horse has runny eyes: what can this indicate?

A number of problems can cause a discharge from the eyes. Any source of inflammation, pain or infection can cause a discharge that results from increased tear and fluid production associated with the eyes.

Also, blockage of the tear ducts (which normally drain the tears directly into the nose) can result in the overflow of tears down the face. Whatever the cause, it is important to address it promptly, as eye problems can rapidly progress beyond the point where they respond fully to treatment, and vision can be affected in the long term.

A veterinary examination should allow diagnosis of the source of the problem. This may include examination of the membranes surrounding the eye, ophthalmoscopy of the eye (which can be aided by local anaesthesia of the area), and the application of fluorescent dye to the surface of the eye. The latter shows up damaged areas on the cornea (the front of the eye), and also tests the patency of the tear

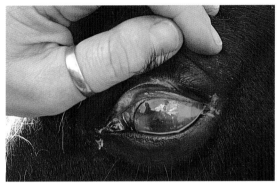

■ This ocular injury is shown up clearly by application of fluorescent dye.

ducts, as it should arrive at the nostril on the same side within five minutes or so. Tests may identify inflammation and infection of the ocular membranes (for example, conjunctivitis), allergies, ocular injuries, and other abnormalities of the eyes such as foreign bodies or even tumours.

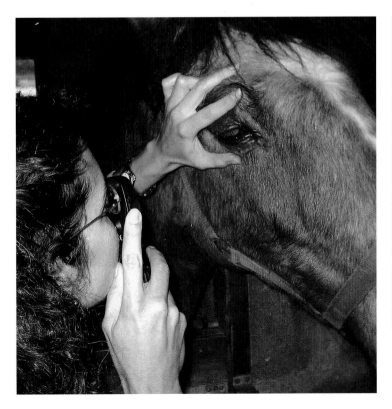

TREATMENT

Treatment may include:

➤ use of topical medicines (see How to apply eye medication page 71);

➤ flushing of blocked tear ducts;

➤ or even surgery.

➤ In addition tear overflow can scald the hair and skin beneath the eyes, and it also attracts flies that can introduce further infection, so it is important to clean away any discharge regularly with cooled boiled water on clean cotton wool.

➤ Vaseline can also be used to protect the skin beneath the eyes.

■ An ophthalmoscope allows the vet to make a thorough examination of a horse's eye.

My horse has scabby bits inside her ears: is this significant?

Ear problems are relatively rare in horses, but even apparently minor problems can cause reduced performance due to sensitivity of the area and headshaking (Headshaking p92). Loss of hearing and balance are also potential results of ear problems, though these are rarely seen.

Masses and tumours can develop associated with the ears, and tooth cysts can occur and cause tender lumps, which may or may not discharge fluid into or around the ear, causing irritation and attracting flies. Ear infections may occasionally occur, and ear injuries are sometimes seen. However, the most common lesion that we see associated with the ear is probably that known as 'aural plaques'. These are greyish-white, raised areas usually found on the inner surface of the ear flaps, which often seem to be associated with large numbers of flies and fly irritation. They generally start as one or two small areas, and over time coalesce until they may affect most of the skin on the inner surface of the affected ear or ears. They are thought to result from a papilloma virus, and may be associated with fly bites; however, they rarely cause any problems other than unsightliness.

■ Aural plaques in a horse's ear may attract flies and cause irritation.

TREATMENT

➤ Occasionally topical anti-inflammatory treatment is needed to reduce tenderness in the area.
➤ Most affected horses may benefit from the use of ear hoods when flies are about.

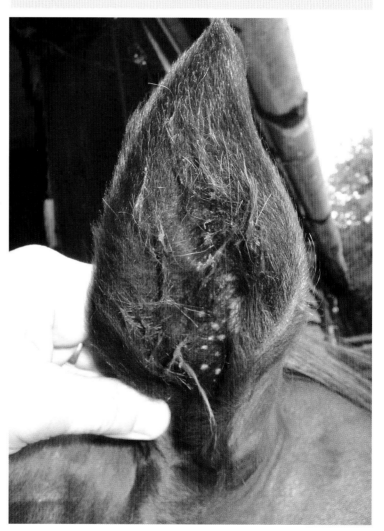

What can cause swellings on the face?

A whole variety of problems can cause facial swelling, ranging from fly bites to a number of more serious conditions. Swelling can obviously follow trauma, even when no skin wound is present, and other potential problems include muscle damage, nerve paralysis, circulatory disorders, tumours, allergies and infections, all of which should be checked promptly by a vet.

Probably the most common cause of facial swelling is an infection of a tooth root or sinus, which can cause painful swellings to develop over the jaws and in the area between the eyes. Similar swellings can result from a horse packing food in the cheek area as a result of having sharp teeth; in such cases quidding (dropping partially chewed mouthfuls of food) is also quite common. Tooth 'bumps' can also form as new teeth are coming through (Dentistry p15), but these do not usually cause problems. Occasionally, tooth tissue can also develop elsewhere on the face as 'dentigerous cysts', which may ooze fluid and cause irritation, and sometimes require surgical removal. Less problematic cysts may develop in the nostrils.

Swelling of the glands at the angle of the jaw and also in the groove between the jaw bones usually indicates infection (and can be associated with strangles (Respiratory disease p96)), although it can also be seen in horses that have salivary swelling due to recently eating spring grass. The head is one of the parts of the body most often affected by tumours and sarcoids, particularly near the eyes. Soft swellings above the eyes may be seen in horses with damage to their chewing muscles, and fatty deposits in this area can cause swellings, most often seen in ponies suffering with Cushing's disease (Cushing's disease p143). Generalized facial swelling may occur due to allergic reactions or to disorders of the circulation (Heart disease p93), strangles, or even because of the over-tight use of a cribbing strap (Vices p50).

Whatever the suspected cause, problems in the head region should be seen promptly by a vet, as early treatment may be needed to ensure the best result is reached.

■ The head must be viewed from the front in order to appreciate any lack of symmetry that may be present due to swellings.

Why does my mare headshake? What can I do?

Headshaking is an extremely frustrating cause of loss of performance. It is usually characterized by sudden, abrupt vertical movements of the head, but also sometimes side-to-side ones, rubbing of the nose on the leg, and other even more bizarre movements. Although in some cases an underlying disease can be found and treated, and some cases are thought to result from nerve pain that follows previous episodes of herpes virus infection (Herpes virus p114), the majority of cases are extremely hard to pin down, and the response to symptomatic treatment can be poor. Around 60 per cent of cases are seasonal in origin, suggesting some kind of environmental cause, perhaps associated with allergies, heat or light, and most of these sadly get worse with time.

In all cases, a thorough check-up is advisable to see if there are any underlying causes, which, if found, can be treated. It is also worth investigating whether badly fitting or unsuitable tack (Tack p22), or poor riding are causing the condition, and in summer insect repellents should be used to ensure that fly worry (Insects p21) is not involved. A veterinary investigation should include a full examination of the eyes and ears, nose, mouth and face, with particular reference to any abnormalities of the teeth, sinuses and other internal structures. Such an examination usually includes endoscopy (Endoscopy p96) of the nose and throat, and head x-rays and scintigraphy (Scintigraphy p131) can also be

TREATMENT

Where a cause of headshaking is not found, horses may still benefit from symptomatic or experimental treatment.

➤ Some horses seem to be sensitive to sunlight at certain frequencies, and do well with tinted contact lenses or sun visors;

➤ others may respond well to anti-allergic therapy, or medication aimed at reducing inflammation, pain and nerve sensitivity.

➤ A surprisingly high number of these horses (around 70 per cent) seem to benefit from the use of nose nets, although the exact mechanism by which this helps is poorly understood – it may simply be that the sensation of the net on the nose distracts the horse from whatever other irritating sensation it had.

➤ Alternative treatments such as acupuncture (Acupuncture p13) have also been tried in some cases, with variable success.

useful. Blocking the nerves (Nerve blocks p120) that carry sensation from various areas of the face can also be helpful, and if this results in cessation of headshaking, then the nerves can be cut through for a longer-term effect.

■ This pony is wearing a nose net to prevent headshaking.

The vet said my horse has a murmur: should I stop riding her?

A heart murmur is simply an abnormal sound that is heard when listening to the heart. Each time the heart beats there are normally four main sounds associated with its activity, although it isn't always possible to hear all of them. Listening through the stethoscope the heart sounds like b-lub-dub-da b-lub-dub-da, if all four sounds are heard. Contraction or pumping of the heart (systole) occurs between the lub and dub sounds, whilst the filling of the heart ready for the next beat (diastole) occurs between the dub and lub sounds.

Systolic murmurs (those heard during heart contraction) generally relate to abnormal or turbulent flow of blood through 'holes in the heart' or the atrioventricular valves in the heart. This can result in decreased forward flow of blood with each heartbeat, and reduced circulation. In addition, the backflow of blood can cause fluid to settle out in the lungs and under the skin, causing breathing difficulties (Respiratory disease p96) and oedema. Diastolic murmurs are more often associated with leakage of blood back through the aortic valve, which can also result in cardiac disease.

The difficulty in assessing murmurs is that perfectly normal horses, particularly those that are fit, may also have murmurs that may initially appear concerning, but in fact only relate to changes in the rate of blood flow and are not associated with disease. In addition, many horses that do have mild disease associated with murmurs can cope with a

What is echocardiography?

An ultrasound scanner can be used to make an image of the heart on a screen in 'live' real time. The contractions of the heart can be seen, and rates of flow of blood through the heart can be measured. This allows evaluation of the size of the heart, the healthiness of the heart muscles and valves, and the degree to which the heart contracts as it pumps. Structural abnormalities of the valves can also be picked up, and holes in the heart can be seen.

degree of valve incompetence without it affecting their ability to perform whatsoever.

This means that the detection of a murmur *per se* does not necessarily mean that a horse should no longer be ridden, or that it is unable to perform at all, or at its intended level. Instead, it is important that murmurs are characterized as to their likely cause and severity so that an accurate assessment of their significance can be made; this sometimes necessitates further investigation, for example by re-examining after exercise using ECG and echocardiography. Some horses with murmurs can continue to enjoy good health and work safely.

■ Thorough auscultation (listening with a stethoscope) of the heart can allow the identification of heart murmurs and some arrythmias.

What symptoms do heart problems cause in horses?

It is actually relatively rare to see any signs of heart problems in horses at all. Severe heart conditions are reasonably uncommon in horses, and most can tolerate a low level of heart problems with little in the way of signs of disease. However, signs that *can* be seen include reduced performance and energy, as well as an increased breathing rate. Swellings may form in the lower parts of the body – the limbs and under the tummy – and in severe cases other symptoms are seen: difficulty breathing (Respiratory disease p96), coughing, and signs of poor circulation such as cool extremities. On more detailed examination it may be noted that affected horses have an increased heart rate at rest (Examining your horse pp57–8), and that their heart rate after exercise is extremely high and stays high for much longer than that of a normal horse. A prolonged capillary refill time is another indicator of poor circulation, and in severe cases, the mucous membranes may even have a bluish tinge. Collapse and death due to heart disease is, thankfully, extremely rare.

Heart problems can occur in all ages and types of horse. Some developmental abnormalities can be seen in foals causing these sorts of symptoms, whilst adult horses can suffer from heart disease associated with arrhythmias (abnormal heart rhythm) or valve disorders (which cause murmurs). Heart murmurs (Murmurs pp93) may be picked up when listening to the heart at rest or after exercise, as also may arrhythmias. However, identification of a murmur (an abnormal heart sound) or an arrhythmia does not necessarily mean that a horse has an associated problem: some may be associated simply with a high degree of fitness, and even if associated with disease, others may be well tolerated by the affected horse. In either case, it is extremely important to determine the exact problem. Diagnosis may necessitate ECG, cardiac ultrasonography (Echocardiography p93) and chest radiography, as well as a thorough clinical examination at rest and after exercise, and it should help in the assessment of whether the affected horse can cope with its level of exercise or not, and whether or not it poses a risk to its rider. Where treatment is necessary, it should be carried out promptly to give horses the best chance of recovery.

What is ECG (see illustration below)?

Electrocardiography (ECG) involves attaching electrical leads to the horse's skin, which pick up the electrical activity of the heart. A trace is formed showing the impulses passing through the different parts of the heart, and this can give useful information about the activity of the pacemaker (which initiates each heartbeat), the transmission of electrical impulses through the heart to make it pump properly, and the general healthiness of the heart tissue. It is particularly useful for picking up arrhythmias, but can also give helpful information in other types of heart disease. To allow an ECG to be taken at exercise, or over long periods of time to pick up intermittent problems, radiotelemetry can be used, which involves the leads on the heart being attached to a radio transmitter (which can be attached to the tack or surcingle); the information is then transmitted to the radio-receiver where the ECG trace is formed. Alternatively a small computerized ECG unit can be used: this stores long periods of information that can be analysed later.

■ An ECG trace shows the electrical activity of the heart. Abnormalities in rhythm and function can be identified.

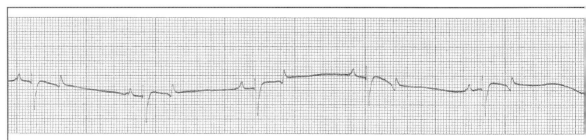

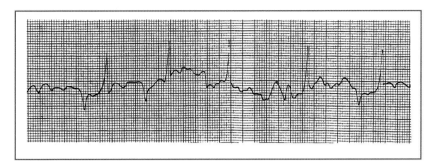

■ Atrial fibrillation: this racehorse's pacemaker has stopped working properly resulting in an irregular heartbeat and poor performance.

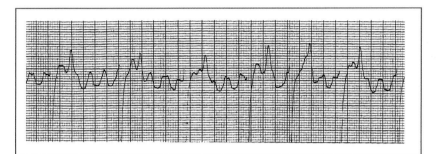

■ Atrial flutter: lack of normal pacemaker activity results in an uncontrolled, irregular heartbeat and lethargy.

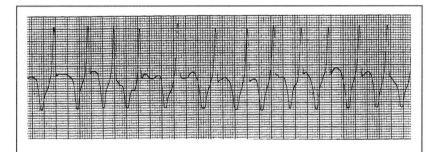

■ Ventricular tachycardia: a rapid, irregular heartbeat which can be associated with collapse.

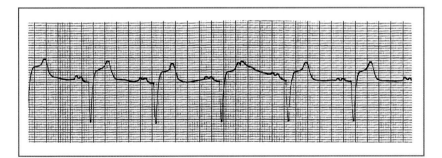

■ Sinus rhythm: after medication the horse's heart is beating normally.

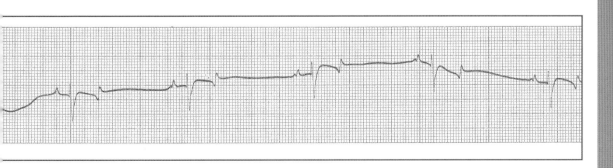

Why does my horse have difficulty breathing, and cough on exercise?

Respiratory disease is one of the most common causes of poor performance in horses, and respiratory function is usually the factor that limits levels of performance even in apparently healthy horses. This means that a fully functional respiratory system is particularly important for those horses that compete at a high level. Even a level of respiratory compromise that causes no signs of disease can limit a horse's ability to ventilate its lungs, thus reducing its tolerance for exercise.

Clinical symptoms of overt respiratory disease include breathing difficulties, coughing, nasal discharge and loss of energy. Such symptoms may also be seen in horses with severe cardiovascular disease due to the build-up of fluid in the lungs, and poor circulation (Heart disease p93).

Allergies (Allergies p81), infections, abnormal laryngeal function (Laryngeal problems p100), disease of the pharynx (back of the throat) or larynx (opening of the windpipe), and tumours can also be involved, as can bleeding from the lungs during strenuous exercise (exercise-induced pulmonary haemorrhage, or EIPH). Diagnosis is aided by a thorough clinical examination, endoscopy (often before *and* after exercise, and sometimes during exercise on a treadmill: endoscopy, right), and in some cases radiography (Radiography p121) and ultrasonography (Ultrasonography p112).

What is endoscopy?

Endoscopy involves passing a fibreoptic tube into a horse so that internal structures can be seen. Endoscopes can be inserted into several parts of the body including the bladder, the uterus and the stomach, but are most often used to investigate respiratory disease. In such cases, the endoscope is passed up the horse's nose, examining the nasal passages, and structures in the throat (including the sinus openings, guttural pouches, and structure and mobility of the larynx). It can also be passed down into the lungs, and the internal surface of the lungs examined for discharges, which, if present, can be sampled. It allows diagnosis of a range of respiratory diseases including laryngeal paralysis, guttural pouch and sinus disease, and respiratory allergies, infections and sources of bleeding.

What are RAO, COPD and SPAOPD?

■ Oil-seed rape is a common cause of allergic respiratory disease.

These acronyms all apply to the same basic disease: whether you call it recurrent airway obstruction (RAO), chronic obstructive pulmonary disease (COPD), or summer pasture-associated obstructive pulmonary disease (SPAOPD), you are talking about an allergic respiratory disease of the horse that is characterized by breathing difficulties. In all cases an allergic response (usually to an inhaled substance such as dust or pollen) causes inflammation within the airways, which reduces their elasticity and causes the development of inflammatory fluid. This in turn causes a cough, nasal discharge, and an increased effort of breathing. The latter can cause hypertrophy (overdevelopment) of the abdominal muscles due to their increased workload in breathing, with the development of a resultant muscle ridge on the horse's side, known as a 'heaves line'.

The most usual culprits are the dust and fungal spores found in hay and bedding, and even tiny amounts of dust can cause a significant ongoing response. Although most affected horses do best managed outside in the fresh air, some are sensitive to pollens (and that of oil-seed rape seems to be a particularly common source of problems), and for these, stabling on dust-free bedding during summer may be a better option.

Diagnosis can include analysis of fluid retrieved from the respiratory system during endoscopy, and even blood allergy testing.

TREATMENT

Medical treatments include:

➤ bronchodilators (drugs that dilate the airways to assist breathing);

➤ mucolytics (to break down mucus and allow it to be coughed out more easily);

➤ steroids (to reduce airway inflammation); and

➤ where necessary, antibiotics (to treat secondary infections).

Some medicines may be best given orally or by injection (Giving medication p72), but in most cases the best results are derived from giving medicines directly into the lungs using a metered dose inhaler (a human inhaler) together with a spacer device (*below*), or even by means of a nebulizer.

My mare has a nasal discharge: what might be the cause?

Discharge from the nose can originate from the nasal passages, throat, lungs, or even stomach, and may have a number of causes. Unilateral nasal discharge – one nostril only – normally comes from the nasal passage on that side, and is caused by problems such as a nasal injury, a sinus problem, or guttural pouch disease, although the latter can cause discharge to come down both nostrils. Bilateral nasal discharge more commonly comes from further back in the horse's body: it can relate to infection or inflammation in the lungs, or to problems in the oesophagus (gullet) or stomach.

The type of nasal discharge can also indicate the cause. Pus usually indicates infection, although it can relate to a primary allergic or inflammatory condition, and it can be caused by tumours. Blood may relate to injuries (such as due to a foreign body, or to minor damage to superficial blood vessels following the insertion of a stomach tube or endoscope), or it can issue from tumours, or from the lungs after over-exertion. Food material (grass or frothy short feed) usually indicates either choke (Choke p61) or severe colic (Colic p102).

A snotty nose, together with other signs of infection such as swollen glands, a high temperature and malaise, usually relate to infectious respiratory diseases such as flu, herpes virus or strangles. Such symptoms should always be investigated promptly by a vet, and affected horses should be isolated pending confirmation as to whether or not an infectious condition is present.

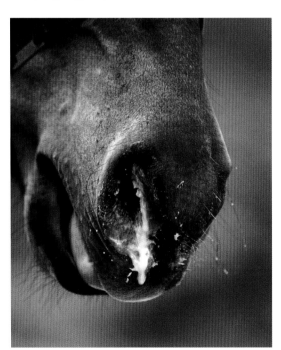

■ Thick discharge from the nose may indicate respiratory infection.

Isolating horses

When an infectious condition is suspected, affected horses should be:

➤ isolated in a box or paddock well away from all other horses.

Handlers should:

➤ use separate grooming and stable equipment;
➤ change their overalls;
➤ wash their hands;
➤ dip their boots in a suitable antiseptic before and after dealing with such horses.

My gelding recently had a nosebleed: what might have caused this?

Causes of nosebleeds include nasal injuries; tumours and infections in the nose, throat and sinuses; fungal infections of the guttural pouch; and EIPH (lung haemorrhage due to over-exertion). It may be possible to get an idea as to the cause from a thorough history. Useful information includes whether the discharge (Nasal discharge p98) was unilateral or bilateral, whether it was clean fresh blood or was mixed with pus, and whether it appeared to occur during or following exercise. A thorough physical examination is also helpful: for instance, sinus problems often cause pain and distortion of the facial bones between the eyes. However, endoscopic examination is necessary for a more accurate diagnosis to be made, and further tests on fluid sampled from the guttural pouches or lungs may be required.

What are the guttural pouches?

The guttural pouches are a dilation in the horse's Eustachian tube – the thin tube that connects ear and throat – containing many of the major nerves involved in swallowing, and also the carotid artery (the main artery to the head). They open into the back of the throat, and bacterial or fungal infections can cause discharge into this area, as well as causing damage to the aforementioned nerves and arteries.

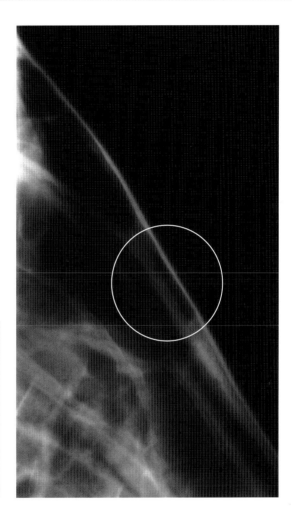

■ Fluid has collected in this horse's sinus as the result of a sinus infection. A severe nasal discharge was evident, containing pus and blood.

My horse sometimes whistles as he breathes: is he a roarer?

A roarer is a horse that makes an abnormal noise during respiration, normally when at a high level of exercise. The characteristic roar or whistle is normally associated with partial paralysis of the larynx, causing it to be unable to open fully during breathing, so that part of it flaps and resonates within the airway as air rushes through.

There are a number of causes for this condition, but the most common is left laryngeal hemiplegia (LLH), a condition that is relatively common in Thoroughbred horses. In affected horses the right side of the larynx functions normally, but the left side is partially or fully paralysed, reducing air flow during breathing to various degrees. Cases are graded from one to six depending on their severity, so that six represents a horse with no mobility at all of its left laryngeal cartilage, which hangs limply into the airway, whilst three might represent a horse whose left laryngeal cartilage is only mildly affected, leaving it with partial mobility.

Other causes of poor performance that may be confused with left laryngeal hemiplegia include structural abnormalities of the larynx such as arytenoid chondritis, and also abnormalities of the epiglottis and soft palate that cause problems such as epiglottic entrapment and dorsal displacement of the soft palate during exercise. These conditions can make horses have difficulty breathing, and can cause abnormal noises such as gulping during exercise. Exact diagnosis of these conditions requires endoscopy at exercise – for example, on a treadmill – so that the mobility of the larynx, epiglottis and soft palate can all be examined while they are functioning at high breathing rates.

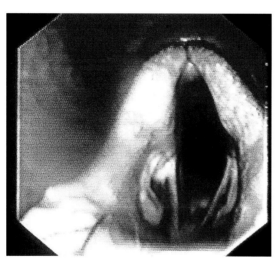

■ Endoscopy may be necessary to investigate abnormalities of the larynx.

TREATMENT

Depending on the severity in each case, affected horses may not be able to perform at their intended level without treatment. Treatments include:

➤ A 'tieback' operation, which involves tying the affected cartilage back out of the airway: this aids breathing, but it can make horses more likely to inhale food during swallowing, and can therefore cause other problems.

➤ Other surgical methods can also be used, including tracheostomy, which allows the horse to breathe through a hole in his neck, bypassing the larynx altogether.

Is lungworm a risk if I graze my horse in a field with donkeys?

It is commonly said that horses and donkeys should not be grazed together because of the risk of lungworm causing respiratory disease. The basis to this is that donkeys are relatively resistant to disease due to lungworm, whilst horses are much more susceptible, and donkeys (and tapirs) can pass worms to horses whilst appearing healthy themselves. This means that horses grazed with donkeys, or on pasture used by donkeys within the previous year or so, may be exposed to lungworm (even if the donkeys appeared healthy), with consequent development of a cough, nasal discharge and increased effort of breathing. However, lungworm is relatively easy to prevent with anthelmintics (Worming p17), and any wormer

■ Donkeys, mules and ponies can be co-grazed as long as they are regularly wormed with a wormer effective against lungworm.

containing a macrocyclic lactone (for example, ivermectin/ moxidectin) is normally effective. Regular worming of donkeys and horses therefore obviates the need for concern, and allows donkeys and horses to be co-grazed safely.

If lungworm is suspected as a cause of respiratory disease it can be confirmed following examination of dung samples (the infective larvae are passed in faeces), or it may be picked up on examination of fluid sampled from the lungs.

What types of colic are life-threatening? Can any be avoided?

Because the initial signs of colic (abdominal pain) generally bear little relation to the severity of the underlying problem, and as some cases of colic are life-threatening, it is important to call for urgent veterinary attention if any signs of colic are seen (Colic p61). Causes of colic range from a low-grade impaction to twisted and damaged gut that can lead to toxaemia and death within hours. This means that whilst some cases respond well to medication that relieves pain and gut spasm and keeps the horse hydrated, others might require emergency surgical treatment if death is to be avoided, or prompt euthanasia (Euthanasia p74) if surgical treatment is not an option.

■ Violent rolling is typical in a horse with colic as he tries to relieve his discomfort.

DIAGNOSING COLIC

The role of the attending vet is to try to determine the type and severity of colic that is present so that mild cases can be treated at home, while those cases that are more serious, recurrent, or for which the cause cannot be immediately diagnosed, are referred into a hospital facility. Clinical examination can yield a great deal of information:

➤ A heart rate (Examination pp57-8) consistently above 60 beats per minute is a sign of a serious problem, and assessment of the circulation and the mucous membranes is also helpful.
➤ During rectal examination it may be possible to feel which area of the gut is involved, what type of problem has occurred, and whether or not the bowel is displaced or twisted.

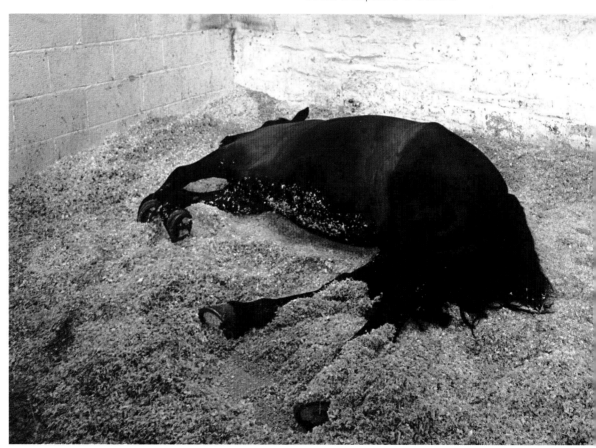

➤ Passage of a stomach tube via the nose can allow the stomach contents to be siphoned out, resulting in decompression of the stomach and assessment of whether or not a severe small bowel problem is present. The presence of spontaneous nasal reflux (where the stomach contents come down the nose: Nasal discharge p98) indicates a severely distended stomach and a very serious problem involving the small intestine.

➤ The sampling of peritoneal fluid (which surrounds the abdominal organs) from the abdomen can also be helpful: turbid or bloody peritoneal fluid indicates that the bowel is unhealthy and that surgery may be indicated.

➤ Blood tests, abdominal ultrasound (Ultrasonography p112) and laparoscopy give further information, although in some severe cases the quickest way to diagnose and treat cases of colic is to proceed to surgery rapidly: those horses that clearly have a major problem may be best opened up as soon as possible to allow diagnosis and give the best chance of treatment being early and effective.

AVOIDING COLIC

Some cases of colic are avoidable, whilst others are not and simply reflect bad luck. In general the chances of colic may be reduced if the following parameters are observed:

➤ Feeding horses a consistent diet with sufficient forage and not too much starch (in the form of concentrates) helps avoid colic (Feeding p24), and aiming for a generally good state of health without too much stress is also helpful.

➤ Changes in diet are often linked with colic and so should be avoided. Increasing the energy levels in rations is a common trigger, but cutting them down can be just as problematic, particularly in the case of injured horses that are suddenly put on to box rest with reduced concentrate feeds, and take to eating their bedding (Bedding p49) out of hunger and boredom. This is probably one of the most usual causes of impactions, and can be avoided by using non-palatable bedding material, feeding fresh cut grass, and providing plenty of hay and lots of toys.

➤ Feeding greedy horses on short grass can also cause problems. Overgrazing results in horses swallowing large amounts of earth and sand, which can cause bowel irritation, diarrhoea and bowel blockage (sand colic: Feeding p23). In areas of light sandy soil where this is a problem, prophylactic use of psilium husk in the diet (a dose rate of 150g Isogel/ 500kg horse in feed once weekly has been advised by some practitioners) can help to avoid the build-up of sand in the bowels.

■ To find out if there is sand in a horse's faeces, mix a sample of its dung with water in a bucket, swirl it round, then pour most of it away whilst continuing to turn the bucket: any sand will remain at the bottom of the bucket. This allows early recognition of horses that are at risk of developing sand colic and need preventative treatment.

➤ Worms (Worming p17) are a common cause of colic: strongyles can cause disruption of bowel circulation, abnormal bowel motility, and abdominal damage and pain; tapeworms may also cause abnormal bowel motility, and even bots can be a problem. Cyathostomes (redworms) can cause diarrhoea and colic, and roundworms gut blockage, particularly in young horses. Regular worming is therefore of paramount importance in the avoidance of colic and other diseases.

What can you do to avoid colic?

➤ avoid stresses and changes in management;
➤ avoid dietary changes;
➤ feed a forage-based diet;
➤ avoid overgrazing or use psilium husk in food where this cannot be avoided;
➤ worm regularly.

How can I avoid my horse getting choke?

Choke, or oesophageal obstruction, usually occurs as a one-off life-threatening condition (Choke p61) due to a blockage forming in the oesophagus after the horse has swallowed items that are poorly chewed. Unsoaked sugar beet is a common culprit, so sugar beet should always be well soaked (usually for twenty-four hours), and buckets of soaking sugarbeet should be covered and kept in a feed room to prevent access by greedy horses. Poorly chopped carrots and other vegetables can also be involved, and it is always advisable to chop vegetables lengthways rather than across, as this decreases the chance of choking.

Other causes of choke include:

➤ Greed: some horses will choke simply because they eat too fast; these greedies will benefit from having their food dampened, and toys put in their bowls for them to eat around.

➤ Others may choke because they have problems with swallowing (dysphagia), or suffer from abnormalities of the oesophagus – indeed, some horses with underlying problems of this type will have repeated episodes of choke, characterized by difficulty swallowing and food material such as grass appearing at the nose.

➤ The causes of dysphagia include damage to the nerves (Neurological disease p140) and muscles that are involved in swallowing, and this can occur following injuries, infections and guttural pouch diseases (Guttural pouches p99).

➤ Swallowing disorders, choke and the nasal regurgitation of food can also be associated with grass sickness, a digestive disorder associated with eating grass containing a factor that damages bowel function (Feeding p23) and causes acute or chronic colic (Colic p102).

➤ Oesophageal problems such as narrowing or stricture formation may follow previous episodes of choke, or may be associated with other types of disease of the neck.

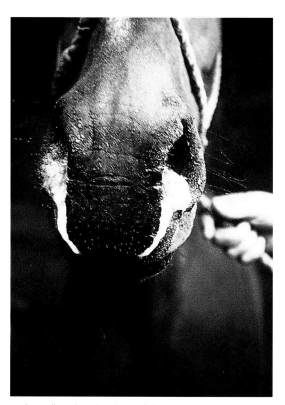

■ As well as showing signs of distress the horse with choke may produce a nasal discharge.

MANAGEMENT

➤ Diagnosis of the causes of choke can be made following endoscopy (Endoscopy p96) of the throat and oesophagus, and sometimes radiography is also helpful.

➤ Any horse that is predisposed to choke and has repeated episodes of choke may need a grass-based diet (horses rarely choke on grass).

➤ Hay and dry forage should be avoided (Feeding p23), and any short feeds should be soaked to form a mash/ gruel to aid swallowing.

What causes diarrhoea, and how can it be treated?

Foal heat diarrhoea commonly occurs due to changes in the milk when the mare has her first season after foaling. Whilst mild cases may not require treatment, severe cases, like this one, do.

Like colic, diarrhoea can have a range of different causes, but one of the most common is worms (Worming p17).

Other causes of diarrhoea include:

➤ nutritional changes (for example, foal heat diarrhoea seen in the foal when the dam has her first season after foaling and changes in the milk occur);

➤ bacterial and viral infections;
➤ some types of medical therapy;
➤ inflammatory disease of the bowel;
➤ bowel tumours.

Diagnosis may be achieved following clinical examination, but faecal tests, blood tests, intestinal absorption tests, and even examination of gut biopsy samples may also be needed.

TREATMENT

Initial therapy is usually directed at:

➤ providing a relatively bland diet (it helps to cut out lush grass, short feeds and carrots);

➤ stopping any medicines that may be involved;

➤ and giving probiotics, which help to re-balance gut bacteria.

➤ Various absorbents may also be used, medication that slows gut motility may also be helpful, and ensuring that affected horses are wormed appropriately is obviously very important.

Antibiotics and immune stimulants may be indicated in some cases, and those horses that don't respond well to initial therapy may also benefit from anti-inflammatory medicines. However, some cases of diarrhoea can be very hard to settle down in the long term.

Peritonitis can be fatal: what is it, and can it be treated?

Peritonitis literally means inflammation of the peritoneum – the membrane that coats the bowels and the other organs and lines the abdomen. Inflammation and infection of the peritoneum can follow some types of infection, immune suppression, breeding and foaling injuries, rectal injuries, colic and abdominal surgery. Whatever the cause, the result is that the peritoneum stops being smooth and becomes rough and sticky so that areas of bowel may become stuck together, causing adhesions. This affects organ and bowel function, and can result in severe abdominal pain. Leakage of fluid and bacteria through the damaged peritoneum also contributes to further inflammation and pain. Other symptoms include weight loss, depression, anorexia, and high temperatures.

TREATMENT

Depending on the cause, treatment may include:

➤ intensive medical and fluid therapy; or

➤ it may necessitate surgery to attempt to remove infected tissue and prevent bowel leakage.

The problem with peritonitis in those horses that have already undergone surgery is that it may be associated with a generally weakened immune system. Unless a specific problem such as a leaky area of bowel is suspected or confirmed, requiring further surgical treatment, supportive medical therapy may be the only option and, particularly in those horses that were already very sick at the time of surgery, this may not always be successful.

■ Abdominal surgery may be necessary in the case of peritonitis.

I just can't get weight on my horse. What can I do?

A whole range of factors can be involved in causing weight loss or poor weight gain. Age is often a factor, but even in young horses low bodyweight can be associated with insufficient feeding (Feeding p24), poor teeth (Dentistry p15), digestive disorders, worms, liver (Liver disease p109), kidney or heart disease (Heart disease p93), some types of cancer, and, in fact, almost any disease.

Where affected horses are apparently healthy, the first step is to make sure that the horse's general management is up to scratch: make sure he is wormed up to date (Worming p17); fed sufficiently and appropriately for his type and his exercise regime (Feeding p24); and get his teeth checked (Dentistry p15). Rugging him up to help him conserve heat and therefore energy may also be advisable. Objective monitoring of weight with regular monthly weight-taping (Weight management p24) allows an assessment of whether a thin horse is gaining or losing weight.

Those horses that seem unwell, are lethargic, or don't respond to initial management changes, should, however, be investigated further. A thorough clinical examination may exclude a number of types of disease, or it may indicate an area that needs even further assessment. Also, faecal tests can enable the identification of any parasites present and some digestive disorders, and blood tests to check liver, kidney, muscle and digestive function can also be very helpful.

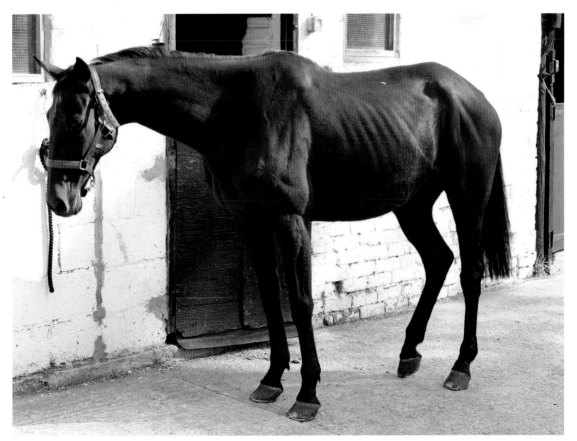

■ Assess your horse's general management when determining the cause of weight loss. Is his worming programme and dental care up to date?

How dangerous is ragwort? How do I deal with it?

Ragwort is a plant that is extremely poisonous to horses (Poisonous plants p44) and one that can be very hard to get rid of: the seeds can travel for very long distances, and with a high germination rate, fields can rapidly become overrun with it. Whilst most horses don't like the taste of it and will only eat the growing plant if they don't have access to enough food, this cannot be relied upon, since some horses seem to develop a taste for it and will seek it out. Ragwort causes more of a problem when dried in hay, as horses can't easily avoid it and may inadvertently eat relatively large amounts.

Within the body, ragwort affects the liver, causing cell damage and loss of function. Although the liver is extremely good at functioning even with high levels of damage (up to 70 per cent of the liver can be non-functional before signs of disease are seen) and is very good at healing, chronic long-term exposure to low levels of ragwort, or sudden exposure to a large amount, can result in a horse suddenly showing signs of liver failure (Liver disease p109). Since the damage caused by ragwort poisoning is irreversible, this can result in long-term disease or death, and every year numerous horses (around 300 a year are diagnosed in the UK, but many more cases go unrecognized) die needlessly of ragwort poisoning.

Avoidance of this poisonous plant is therefore of paramount importance. Fields can be sprayed or topped, but this is rarely very effective, and it must also be remembered that wilted plants remain toxic. In many cases it is far more effective to dig up and remove whole plants before they flower, and to remove and burn the debris to prevent horses coming into contact with wilted plants. Hay should always be bought from a reputable supplier, and any signs of ragwort in hay necessitates disposing of the entire batch.

■ Whilst horses will usually avoid ragwort, they may eat it if they are hungry, or if it is in their hay. Be sure to dig up the whole plant quickly in order to avoid it spreading.

How can we find out if my horse has a liver problem?

Liver disease can occur for a number of reasons, ranging from infection to ragwort poisoning. Hyperlipidaemia (high fat levels in the blood) may also cause liver damage, occurring when a high fat diet is fed to susceptible horses, or when fat ponies are suddenly starved (Feeding p24), resulting in high levels of fat being released into the bloodstream. For this reason food restriction in laminitic ponies (Laminitis p122) should be achieved in a controlled manner, rather than by sudden starvation.

Symptoms of liver disease can vary from mild signs of malaise associated with low-grade chronic disease, to sudden, severe and potentially fatal symptoms associated with acute disease. Symptoms include weight loss (Weight loss p107), chronic diarrhoea (Diarrhoea p105), lethargy (Lethargy p141) and behavioural changes as well as bleeding disorders (Blood diseases p62), colic (Colic p102), loss of balance, head pressing, collapse, fitting (Neurological disease p140), and sudden death.

Investigation

➤ Investigation of such horses is usually based on blood tests: this can show up enzymes released by damaged liver cells, as well as enzymes and toxins that arise in liver disease.
➤ Bile acid levels can also be checked, as these give a fairly accurate guide as to how well the liver is able to function at the time, and blood clotting can also be checked.
➤ Further tests include taking a liver biopsy, which can be done in the standing horse through the abdominal wall, guided by an ultrasound scan. This can give important information regarding the cause and severity of liver damage, as well as the prognosis.

■ A blood sample is taken from the jugular vein. Its analysis can reveal anaemia, infection and liver disease.

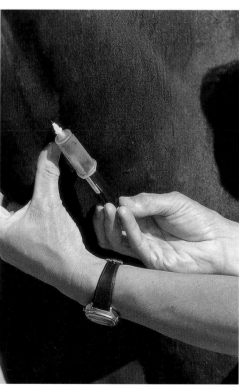

Do I really have to clean my gelding's sheath? He hates it: any tips?

Unfortunately the smegma and dead skin that collect on the surface of the penis have been shown to be potentially carcinogenic (cancer causing), and so it is advisable to clean the penis and sheath regularly. Some geldings, colts and stallions will allow cleaning of the sheath with few problems, and with these it may be cleaned approximately once monthly; others resent their owners even attempting to clean their genitalia, and may need to be sedated. For such horses regular cleaning may not be practicable, but it is a good idea to clean them if they are sedated for any other reason, and particularly if the penis is seen to be covered in old skin and smegma.

When tumours in this area occur, they may be seen as warty or smooth masses that grow on the external or internal surface of the sheath, or on the penis itself. Masses may prevent a horse from being able to drop his penis out to urinate, resulting in difficulty urinating, or messy urination. It is therefore a good idea to make a point of occasionally observing male horses when they are urinating, to check that their genitalia appear normal and that they can urinate normally. If any problems are seen or suspected, a veterinary check-up is advisable.

■ However disagreeable your horse finds it, it is important for his health that you keep his sheath clean.

Cleaning a male horse's genitalia

There are a number of different ways to clean the sheath and penis, and it is a matter of finding a regime that is quick, easy and safe, and that your horse doesn't resent too much; the following procedure is a basic guide:

➤ Have ready a bucket of lukewarm, very dilute antiseptic solution, cotton wool or paper towel, gloves, and a lubricant (either obstetric lubricant or baby oil). Wear a riding hat to protect your head. Do not proceed if your horse becomes dangerous.
➤ Stroke under the horse's tummy and down to the sheath, grasp the penis and try to pull it down gently but firmly so that it leaves the sheath.
➤ Maintaining a grip near the base, wash down with warm antiseptic solution.
➤ Apply a little lubricant, such as KY jelly, to the surface and back up into the sheath as this prevents matter adhering to the skin, thus helping to keep it cleaner in the future.

My horse stales all the time: what's wrong with it?

Urinary problems are relatively rare in horses, but occasionally problems with bladder and urinary function do occur. Infections, inflammation, tumour development, injuries, or the development of bladder stones can all affect urination, leading to apparent difficulty urinating, and frequent passage of small amounts of urine. Affected horses, either male or female, may be seen to strain to urinate, and may not be able to produce a strong stream of urine. Alternatively, constant dribbling of urine may be seen, in the absence of the normal stance for urination, and this can result in urine scalding of the skin, skin infections, and problems with flies being attracted to the area (Fly strike p86). In males, the penis may become prolapsed from the sheath due to straining, and this can result in penile damage if not treated promptly by a vet. Other symptoms that may be seen include recurrent low grade colic (Colic p102), and weight loss (Weight loss p107).

Examination of the urine from affected horses may allow identification of blood, cancer cells, or

■ Mare-ish horses may be especially prone to hormonally-enduced behaviour such as staling frequently, but it is wise to thoroughly investigate this behaviour.

crystals within it, although it should be borne in mind that even normal horses' urine appears cloudy and contains some crystals. Further investigation may also include passing a catheter into the bladder, radiographic techniques, ultrasonography (Ultrasonography p112), and endoscopy (Endoscopy p96) of the urethra and bladder.

Other reasons for the apparent frequency of urination can include hormonal and behavioural factors associated with mares being in season. This can be particularly apparent in 'mare-ish' females that over-express seasonal behaviour in such a way that it can affect their performance. Such mares should be investigated to ensure a medical problem is not present and, given that they are otherwise healthy, may be managed with therapy to suppress or prevent them from coming into season.

I want to breed a foal from my mare. What do I need to know?

If thinking of breeding a foal from a favourite mare, the first consideration is whether or not the mare is suitable for breeding. Older mares may not cope well with pregnancy, and can have reduced fertility, so may not be as suitable as younger mares. In addition, it is not advisable to breed from mares that have significant conformational abnormalities (Conformation p6), medical problems, or difficult behaviour. It is a good idea to have a veterinary check of your mare before you even start any breeding plans to be sure that she is suitable and that her reproductive system appears to be functioning normally. Some mares have a sloping conformation of the vulva, such that it becomes readily contaminated with faecal material, which in turn predisposes to low grade infections and infertility. Such mares can have their vulvas partially stitched (a 'Caslicks' operation) to prevent access of faecal material into the vagina, and this will improve their chances of conception.

Choosing the stallion is the next step, and obviously this will depend on the type of foal that is wanted. Again, it is important to choose a stallion that is healthy and has good conformation, and that will give the foal good genetic material.

If the mare is to be served naturally, swabs and smears will need to be taken from her clitoris and uterus, and a blood test carried out to ensure that she does not carry any venereal diseases. The stallion's stud will advise as to what is required in each case. Sometimes these tests identify low grade uterine infections that can cause infertility if not treated appropriately. Such tests may also need to be carried out if the mare is going away to be artificially inseminated, though if she is to stay at home there may be no necessity for such tests.

In order to find out the optimum time for mating or AI (artifical insemination) to happen, ultrasound scans of the mare's uterus and ovaries can be carried out via the rectum. The development of ovarian follicles can be tracked, and service planned around the time of ovulation to give the best chance of conception. Mares that are subfertile, or that need to have the timing of their ovulation controlled in order to fit in with the stallion or with the availability of AI, can also be treated with hormonal medicines that help to control their cycle and which can improve conception rates.

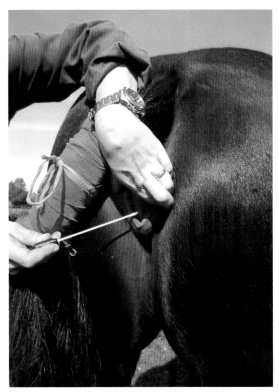

■ Clitoral swabs can allow identification of venereal disease.

What is rectal ultrasonography?

Rectal ultrasound involves inserting a slim ultrasound probe into the rectum within the operator's hand to scan the internal surface of the pelvis and the pelvic organs such as the bladder, uterus and ovaries. It allows evaluation of the reproductive tract, assessment of seasonal activity, and detection of pregnancy.

What are the options for pregnancy diagnosis?

Pregnancy diagnosis can be carried out by rectal examination, blood tests or rectal ultrasonography. Rectal examination can be useful but, depending on the experience of the vet, may only be accurate from around one month of pregnancy, and there may be a period in mid-pregnancy in large mares when the foetus lies too far forward to be easily palpable. Blood tests can identify whether or not pregnancy is present from around 45 days post service onwards, but there is a window between 90 and 120 days in a pregnancy when they can be inaccurate due to changing hormone levels.

In most cases, ultrasound scanning is the most useful way to detect pregnancy, not only because it can be accurate from around 14 days post service, but also because it is the only method that allows

■ Blood tests can be carried out from about 45 days after the mare is covered, before she is obviously pregnant.

twin pregnancies to be detected. Since most horses (particularly thoroughbreds) can't carry twins to term, and the incidence of twin ovulations and thus twin pregnancies in thoroughbreds is relatively high, it is important to detect them before around three weeks of pregnancy so that one can be removed, allowing the other a chance of survival. Further scans are usually carried out at about 25 to 30 days of pregnancy to check that the embryo is developing normally and has a heartbeat, and a further scan or blood test is usually carried out in later pregnancy to check that the mare has not miscarried.

What causes mares to miscarry? How can I protect my mare?

A certain number of pregnancies are lost in the first few weeks due to causes that can't be prevented, such as the development of a non-viable foetus. However, some causes of miscarriage are easily preventable and these include twinning (by Pregnancy diagnosis p113), viral infections (Herpes vaccination pp19–20), bacterial infections and venereal diseases (Preparation for pregnancy p112), fungal infections, hormonal dysfunction, poor nutrition, and access to certain plants and some medicines.

A number of measures can therefore be taken to help avoid abortion:

➤ Swabs taken at the time of service ensure that venereal diseases that can cause abortion are not present. They can also exclude low grade endometritis that can later cause bacterial abortion.

➤ Ultrasound scanning should be employed before three weeks of pregnancy to ensure that twin pregnancy has not occurred, so that, if necessary, treatment can be carried out (Pregnancy p113).

➤ Throughout pregnancy, appropriate feeding is obviously important (Feeding p24).

➤ Mares should be kept away from ergot, fescue, sorghum and sudan grasses, as these plants may be implicated in causing abortion.

➤ Pregnant mares should be kept away from any sick horse or horses that have aborted, and isolated from known sources of disease. In addition, mares can be vaccinated against herpes virus, and (in the USA) equine viral arteritis (Vaccines pp19–20) to prevent abortion.

➤ Finally, mares with poor fertility may benefit from hormonal treatment, and so mares that consistently lose pregnancies should be investigated further.

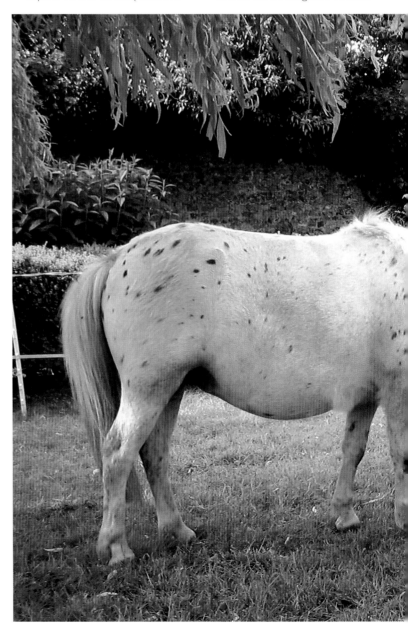

Should a mare sadly lose her pregnancy, it is extremely important to call out the vet promptly, both to check over and blood test the mare and to take samples from the foetus and placenta. This can allow identification of the cause of abortion, which may have implications for the mare's future fertility and for any other mares (and indeed the stallion) with which she has been in contact.

■ Careful attention to the health of the mare during pregnancy increases the chance of a healthy foal.

Signs of impending abortion

➤ premature development of the milk glands,
➤ running of milk,
➤ relaxation of the vulva, and
➤ the production of a vulval discharge.
➤ In addition, depending on the cause of abortion, the mare may be unwell and run a high temperature (Examination p57) around the time of abortion.

How can I prepare for my mare's foaling?

A number of things need to be borne in mind when getting ready for foaling, in order to give the mare and foal the best chance of coming through the process without problems.

➤ It is important to move the mare to the place where she will foal around six weeks before her expected foaling date, so that she can develop immunity appropriate to her surroundings and pass it on to the foal in her milk.

➤ It is also advisable to boost her flu and tetanus vaccinations (Vaccines pp19–20) 4–6 weeks before foaling so that she has a high level of immunity to pass to the foal.

➤ If the mare has had her vulva stitched (Caslicks operation p112) it is advisable to remove the stitches about two weeks before her due date, or before then if signs suggest she may foal early, to prevent her tearing.

➤ Throughout pregnancy adequate food (Feeding p24) and light exercise are essential.

➤ In late pregnancy mares should be managed in clean grassy paddocks by day, and large clean straw stables at night. Both should be carefully checked to ensure there are no potential dangers.

SIGNS OF IMPENDING BIRTH

Signs of impending birth include bagging up (udder development) within the fortnight before birth, enlargement of the teats within around one week of birth, and waxing up (development of a waxy secretion on the teats) within a few days of birth. In addition the vulva and associated ligaments relax within a week of birth, and the vulva may appear suddenly to elongate. If milk is seen to run or drip excessively from the teats before foaling, it may mean that the mare is losing her colostrum (the first milk, which confers immunity on the foal), and this can result in the foal having little or no protection against disease. In such cases the mare's milk should be collected and frozen (if possible), or a colostrum substitute provided for the foal. Otherwise further treatment such as a plasma transfusion (the transfer of blood immune products from mare to foal) may be necessary for the foal.

FOALING DOWN

Early indications of foaling (which usually occurs in the middle of the night) include loss of appetite, and symptoms of mild colic (Colic p102), in which case it is a good idea to make sure the mare is on her own, and to put a tail bandage on her. Labour progresses rapidly, the mare sweating and straining for about half an hour until the waters break, which is followed by strong contractions and the birth of the foal

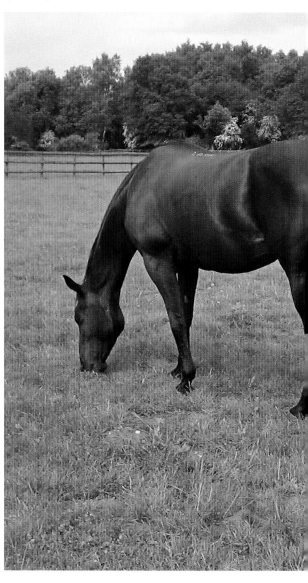

(front feet and nose first) within about 30 minutes. The bag normally breaks as the foal is born. Soon after the birth the mare should get to her feet and lick the foal, and they start to bond, and within an hour or so the foal should also be on its feet. The foal usually starts to suck within three hours of birth, and the afterbirth is normally passed within this time.

Even if all goes well, it is still important to have the vet out within 24 hours of foaling to check the mare and foal over, give the foal a tetanus vaccine (Tetanus p85), and to check that the afterbirth has been passed complete. It is also important to treat the foal's navel with antiseptic at birth and several times within the first 48 hours of birth in order to prevent infection.

Coping with and avoiding problems

Problems at foaling may include:
- ➤ the mare straining unduly;
- ➤ the foal suffering a malpresentation (for instance, with one leg back or hindlegs first);
- ➤ the part of the placental bag around the foal's head not being broken immediately; and
- ➤ the afterbirth not being passed promptly or intact.

All these signs can indicate potentially fatal problems, and it is important to call the vet for an emergency visit at the first sign of any problem.

In the meantime there may be things that the owner can do to help matters along.
- ➤ If necessary, correctly presented foals may be pulled in the direction of the mare's hocks, gently and in rhythm with her contractions. However, repositioning a poorly presented foal can be difficult, and this may be best left to the vet.
- ➤ Breaking the bag over the foal's head and clearing his nostrils to assist breathing can also be helpful. However, it is important not to cut or artificially rupture the umbilical cord, as this can cause haemorrhage; nor should any attempt be made to help passage of the afterbirth, as this can lead to tearing and infection.

Signs of post-foaling infection include:
- ➤ a high temperature (Examination pp57–8),
- ➤ anorexia,
- ➤ malaise,
- ➤ failure of milk production, and
- ➤ laminitis (Laminitis p122).

Any sign of abnormalities should be checked promptly by a vet.

A normal equine pregnancy lasts an average of 342 days, but it can often be around 20 days less or more than this.

■ A mare can foal down safely in a large, clean box or a clean, grassy paddock.

Should I have my colt gelded: only one of his testicles is down?

Although colts that are left entire for longer may grow bigger and develop more masculine characteristics and more 'showiness', most colts benefit from being gelded fairly early on, because it allows them to be well socialized with other horses, instead of leading the solitary life of a stallion. Geldings are also easier to handle than colts.

Most owners have their colts gelded as yearlings or two-year-olds. Usually this is carried out with the colt standing but under sedation in field conditions, as this is cheaper and potentially less stressful than surgery at an equine hospital; however, this is only possible where both testicles are fully descended.

Colts' testicles are normally descended well before they are two, although some can come down later. Undescended or 'retained' testicles are problematic for several reasons. If both are undescended, horses that are entire males can be thought to be gelded, with obvious problems associated with sexual and dominant behaviour, and, potentially, unwanted pregnancies. Undescended testicles also have an increased chance of becoming cancerous, and so should always be removed promptly. Hormonal treatment may help to increase the chance of retained testicles descending, but in most cases, colts with undescended testicles need to be referred to a surgical facility in order to be gelded in a sterile operating room under a general anaesthetic.

■ The behaviour of ungelded colts can be difficult, necessitating protective clothing and the use of a Chifney for leading.

My horse is lame: how can the vet find out what's wrong?

The initial step with any horse that is suspected of being lame is a full clinical and lameness examination (Lameness examination p67) that incorporates an assessment of all the limbs at rest and of the gait at different speeds on a firm surface. Examination during lungeing and at ridden exercise can also be useful, and flexion tests (Flexion tests p120) can allow low grade lamenesses to be unmasked.

In most cases this allows identification of the lame limb (or the lamest limb if more than one are affected); however, many cases will require further investigation in order to diagnose accurately the cause of lameness. Regional anaesthesia, also known as nerve and joint blocks (Nerve blocks p120) can be used to deaden the nerves to various areas of the limbs, allowing identification of the area of the limb that contains the source of pain. This area can then be focused on closely, using techniques such as radiography (Radiography p121), ultrasonography (Ultrasonography p112) or MRI (MRI p125) to identify any lesions. Where horses are not very lame, or have inconsistent responses to nerve blocks, thermography (Thermography p126) or scintigraphy (Scintigraphy p130) can allow identification of areas of high blood flow or healing tissue, indicating the site of an injury.

Once the site and type of injury have been identified, the vet can give advice on the best course of treatment. This may comprise rest, or medical or surgical therapy.

■ A thorough examination of the limbs can be helpful.

WHAT ARE FLEXION TESTS?

Flexion tests involve holding one or more joints in one limb in a flexed position, usually for 40–60 seconds, and then immediately having the horse trotted away and back on a firm surface. Problems causing low grade joint stiffness or pain in associated structures may be unmasked, causing overt lameness (a 'positive' flexion test) under these conditions, even if they do not normally do so.

WHAT ARE NERVE AND JOINT BLOCKS?

Local anaesthetic can be injected around the nerves or into the joints, thus deadening pain sensation from particular areas in the limbs (or elsewhere). If a previously lame horse trots up sound after a particular block, this indicates that the source of the pain was affected by that block, allowing identification of the area that was causing the horse pain. This type of investigation works on a 'trial and error' basis if there are no obvious external signs of an injury, and several nerve or joint blocks may need to be done before the pain source is identified.

■ Nerve and joint blocks can allow identification of the source of pain.

What should I do if my gelding gets a nail prick injury?

It is not that uncommon for a horse to sustain a nail injury to the foot. A loose shoe may twist and then be trodden on, a builder's nail may penetrate the foot, or occasionally a farrier's nail may be inserted in error into the sensitive part of the foot. Solar penetration may also be caused by stones, wire or other sharp items, and these are almost always followed by infection (known as 'pus in the foot' or 'sub-solar infection'). Usually, penetrations occur close to the white line at the periphery of the foot, and although severe infection is a possibility, damage to crucial structures is unlikely. Nails that penetrate the mid-portion of the foot, the frog, the frog sulci (grooves), or even the heel area are, however, a potentially more serious problem because they may involve the pedal bone, the navicular bone and bursa, or even the coffin joint.

What is digital radiography?

Radiography involves passing X-rays through a subject to obtain an image that shows up hard tissues such as bone and metal particularly well, but can also image soft tissue to some extent. It is particularly useful for investigating bone-related disease.

Digital radiography involves using a computer plate, rather than a film, to pick up the X-rays that have passed through the subject, and with computer enhancement of images, it allows excellent image quality to be obtained with low levels of X-ray exposure, thus reducing the X-ray radiation and the danger of secondary health problems to the patient and the operatives.

TREATMENT

➤ If a nail is found *in situ*, it should not be removed unless to leave it where it is will cause further injury. Instead, immediate veterinary attention should be sought, and the foot radiographed before removal of the nail in order to see whether or not it is penetrating close to the structures described above.

➤ If such an injury is identified or suspected, further investigation and treatment in an equine hospital is an immediate necessity, because such injuries can prove fatal if they are not treated intensively.

➤ In less serious cases, a vet still needs to be called promptly as anti-tetanus medication (Tetanus p85) may be necessary, the foot may need to be pared and then poulticed (Poulticing p65) to allow release of pus. Medical treatment may also be required.

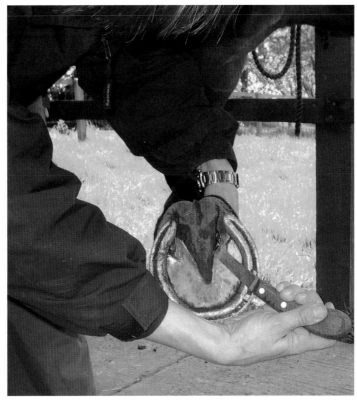

■ Paring the foot with a hoof knife can allow release of infection following an injury caused by the horse treading on a sharp object.

Can you tell me more about laminitis please?

People often imagine that laminitis (meaning inflammation of the laminae that form the junction between the hoof wall and the pedal bone) is a disease of the overweight pony. However, there are nevertheless a number of trigger factors for laminitis, and the disease can be seen in all types of horse.

Laminitis can result from obesity, a sudden overload of starch or carbohydrate (Feeding p24) (usually following accidental access to the feed store), and it can be a consequence of Cushing's disease (Cushing's disease p143). Other factors include excessive concussion on hard ground, overgrown feet with long toes, endotoxaemia (a release of toxins into the blood) following colic (Colic p102) or endometritis (Miscarriage in mares p114), corticosteroid medication (Medication p72), stress, and increased loading of one foot when another is injured. In addition, grass alone can induce laminitis, particularly in spring-time conditions of cold nights and sunny days when fructan levels are high (Feeding p24).

CHARACTERISTIC SIGNS
The condition typically involves pain in both front feet, or at worst, all four feet, with a characteristic shortened 'pottery' gait that is particularly evident on the inside leg as the horse or pony is turned. The affected feet usually feel warm or hot to the touch, and a strong pulse may be felt at the heels (How to feel for a digital pulse p124), indicating inflammation. The application of hoof testers across the sole normally elicits a painful response, and it may be hard to lift any of the feet since increased weight-bearing on the others is resented. In severe and catastrophic cases the pedal bone loosens within the hoof, and a dip may be felt at the coronary band and a bulge seen in the sole due to founder (the sinking or rotation of the pedal bone).

■ To relieve pressure on painful front feet, a laminitic horse will often lean his weight backwards

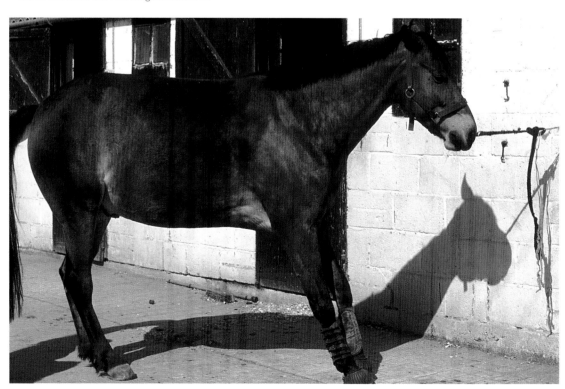

■ Rings on the front wall of the hoof can indicate past episodes of laminitis.

■ Severe laminitis causes the front wall of the pedal bone to rotate away from the hoof wall (the two should be parallel), and can cause the pedal bone to sink within the hoof. Such changes may be untreatable and prove fatal.

TREATMENT

The treatment and management of laminitis includes the following measures:

➤ Radiography (Radiography p121) of the feet allows assessment of whether the pedal bone has rotated or sunk at all within the hoof. It also assists corrective farriery (Farriery p16) in that it can enable the farrier to see how far the toes need to be cut back, and it is a guide as to the individual design of the shoes that will be required to provide support to the frog and pedal bone.

➤ The removal of any identifiable trigger factors, such as reducing food intake, and in particular, the levels of carbohydrate in the diet.

➤ The use of frog supports.

➤ Anti-inflammatory pain-relieving medicines, and medicines that lower the blood pressure in the foot.

➤ Cold hosing may also be helpful.

➤ Box rest on a supportive bedding (for example, sand or deep shavings) is advisable until the animal is sound and off medication, as any exercise will increase the loading of the laminae and can contribute to further damage.

➤ Once the initial phase of the condition is over, corrective farriery to rebalance and, where necessary, support the foot is essential.

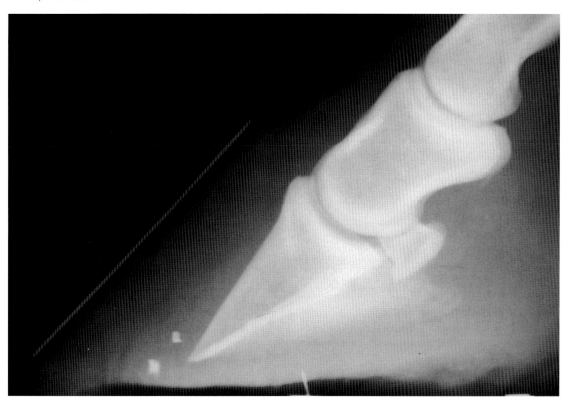

PREVENTIVE MEASURES

Preventive measures include the following:

➤ maintaining the animal on a low calorie diet (Feeding p23);

➤ use of certain antibiotics in feed to suppress the development of the bacteria in the hindgut that cause the release of endotoxins in response to a high carbohydrate diet;

➤ medication for Cushing's disease (Cushing's disease p143) where that is identified.

However, even with the best of treatment, some horses don't make a full recovery, and in some the disease is so severe that euthanasia on humane grounds proves necessary.

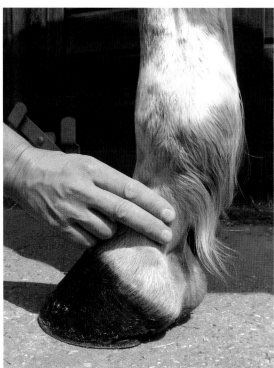

■ Feeling for a digital pulse, which indicates inflammation of the foot and can be apparent in cases of laminitis. The pulse in the palmar digital arteries can be felt at the level of the fetlock or pastern.

How to feel for a digital pulse

It's hard to feel the digital pulse in horses that don't have laminitis, but in those that do, or that have other causes of inflammation in the foot, a 'bounding' pulse may be felt in the digital arteries. These two arteries run down each heel passing over the sesamoid bones at the back of the fetlock, straight down the pastern area to the bulb of the heel. The pulse is most easily felt with a light finger pressure in the mid-pastern area.

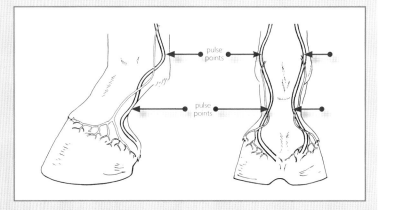

The vet said my horse has palmar foot pain. Is this navicular syndrome?

The term 'palmar foot pain' relates to a diagnosis, made on the basis of clinical examination (Examination pp57–8) and nerve blocks (Nerve blocks p120), that a horse's lameness is due to pain emanating from the structures in the heel area (the palmar foot). These structures include the navicular bone and associated ligaments and bursa, the deep digital flexor tendon, and the coffin joint, and in some cases symptoms relate to navicular disease, a syndrome that can affect all these structures.

This condition is commonly seen as a chronic, progressive, bilateral forelimb lameness in mature horses that typically have low-heeled foot conformation. This type of conformation results

TREATMENT

Treatment involves:

➤ regular farriery to support (or even raise) the heels, reduce concussion in the heel area, and take the strain off the deep digital flexor tendon.

Surgical or medical methods of pain relief can be used, and a variety of other treatments, with varying success rates, may also be employed. However, because the condition is progressive, most horses do well initially with improved farriery alone, but eventually reach a point where they can no longer function and need to be retired or even euthanased due to uncontrollable and worsening lameness.

in excessive stresses passing through all the structures in the heel area, and can lead to damage to any, or all of these structures. Diagnosis of navicular syndrome usually involves a combination of confirmation of palmar foot pain and the identification of typical lesions in the affected feet, which includes changes of bone density within the navicular bone and in the associated structures. In severe cases the navicular bone may even have collapsed or fractured.

One of the problems with diagnosis of navicular syndrome is that many of the changes that may be seen associated with this disease are also seen in some normal, sound horses, and so radiographic findings should be considered carefully along with the results of nerve blocks. Scintigraphy (Scintigraphy p131) and MRI (MRI, *see below*) can also be helpful.

What is MRI?

➤ MRI involves putting the area that is to be imaged within a large magnet, and then recording the magnetic properties of the tissues within. Images are formed on a computer screen, and normally relate to the differing proportions of water in the various tissues. For some types of disease – for example, navicular syndrome – and some areas of the body – for example, the foot – this can give diagnostic images with exceptional clarity of both soft tissues and bony structures.

■ Hoof testers can be used to apply pressure against the sole and the heels, which generally clearly identifies the areas of pain.

My horse has a hot foot: what could be wrong?

Heat in a particular area is one of the signs of inflammation that can indicate the whereabouts of the source of a problem. Heat in the feet can be appreciated by feeling the surface of the hooves or the sole of the foot (though be aware that the hoof surface, particularly of black feet, can become quite warm to the touch if a horse is standing in sunshine). Other signs that help localize a problem in this area include a strong digital pulse in the heel area (How to feel for a digital pulse p124), and the use of hoof testers to apply pressure across the sole; and further investigation including nerve blocks (Nerve blocks p120), radiography (Radiography p121), scintigraphy (Scintigraphy p130) and finally thermography (Thermography, see below) can also be useful. However, even if no obvious signs are seen to localize a lameness, it is always worth bearing in mind that around 90 per cent of lamenesses relate to problems in the foot, so it is a good idea to examine the feet carefully if a horse is lame.

There are a great number of potential causes of lameness in the foot. Those that cause heat include laminitis (Laminitis p122), pus in the foot (Sub-solar infection p121), fracture of the pedal bone, and also some inflammatory conditions of the foot. Pedal bone fractures can occur after surprisingly little obvious external trauma, causing varying degrees of lameness depending on whether the fractures involve the joints or not. Treatment may involve surgery, or supportive farriery and box rest.

Other conditions of the foot include pedal osteitis, or more commonly inflammation of the pedal bone, which can relate to chronic concussion associated with poor conformation; thin soles; insufficient support from the shoes; and excessive work on hard ground. Solar bruises and corns (which occur due to compression under the heels of poorly fitting shoes) can cause similar signs, and sidebone (ossification of the cartilage on either side of the pedal bone, leading to reduced mobility of the coffin joint) also relates to a combination of poor foot balance and excessive concussion, as may navicular syndrome.

CORE TREATMENT

The importance of regular and appropriate farriery (Farriery p16) cannot be overemphasized. Poor foot balance is the main factor involved in the development of many of the causes of lameness that relate to the foot and other structures in the limb, and the correction of foot imbalances is one of the core treatments of lameness.

What is thermography?

Thermography is a form of imaging that picks up the temperatures of superficial structures on the body (for example, the skin). Injuries and inflammation often cause increased blood flow to the affected area, and thus areas of skin heat. These can be imaged on a computer screen, aiding diagnosis.

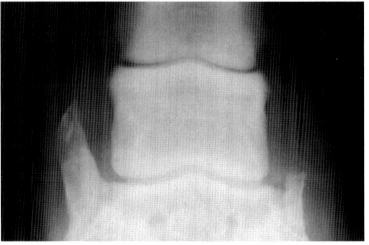

■ Sidebone involves inflammation causing ossification (bony deposits) in the lateral cartilages of the pedal bone, which can reduce coffin joint mobility and cause lameness.

My colt keeps getting his hind leg stuck. What should I do?

The mechanism that allows horses to sleep standing up involves one of the patellar ligaments in the stifle hooking over a notch in the base of the femur, thus holding the hind limb locked straight. Contraction of the muscles in the rump then lifts the patellar ligament free and allows the stifle joint to move again. However, in some young horses that are poorly muscled, recurrent upward fixation of the patella (locking of the kneecap) can be a problem, with the limb locking straight and the horse being unable to move properly. This results in a jerky gait, clicking of the stifle joint, and sometimes swelling in the area. Normally the patella comes free on its own within seconds, but occasionally it remains locked with the limb straight and the toe dragging; then panic can ensue. Emergency treatment involves either pulling the limb out straight in front of the horse whilst pushing the patella in towards the groin, or backing the horse up to allow the patella to come free. However, as horses develop muscle the situation normally sorts itself out, so building fitness is the best treatment for horses that are repeatedly affected. Shoeing the horse with shoes with raised heels can also be helpful. Very occasionally surgical treatment is required.

If a horse's hind limb appears to lock suddenly, this is the most likely cause, and should respond to the treatment described. However, some other conditions of the stifle can cause limb stiffness and poor mobility: these include osteoarthritis (Arthritis p135), OCD (OCD p134) and some injuries. In addition stringhalt, a nervous condition that causes a jerky hind-limb gait, may appear similar. For these reasons, a veterinary check-up is always advisable.

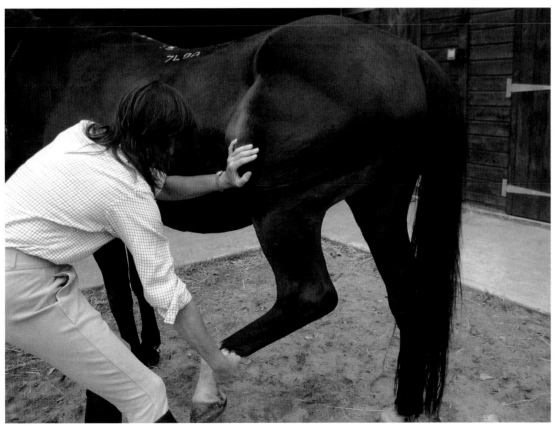

■ A locked patella may be released by pulling the limb forwards whilst pushing inwards on the knee-cap.

Can you tell me more about tendon injuries? How should they be treated?

Between the hoof and the carpus (knee) in the front leg, and the hoof and the hock in the back leg, there are a number of structures that may be loosely referred to as 'tendons'. These include the superficial digital flexor tendon that runs down the back of the limb just under the skin, the deep digital flexor tendon and check ligament that lie just deep to this, and the suspensory ligament that lies even deeper, nestling between the splint bones.

When people refer to a 'pulled tendon', what they usually mean is that one of the structures in this region has been injured. Such an injury commonly follows working at a level beyond the horse's training, or results from an accident in the field or during exercise such as landing badly from a fence,

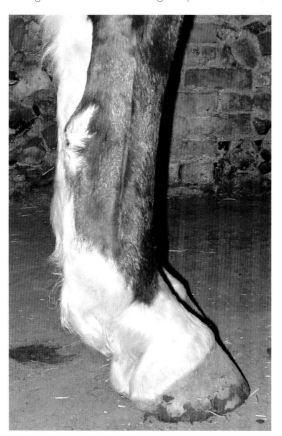

■ A severe tendon injury may result in obvious distortion of the limb and swelling in the area (known as a 'bowed' tendon). More subtle lesions may be difficult to identify.

TREATMENT

Appropriate treatment incorporates:

➤ immediate box rest and prompt veterinary attention;
➤ cool therapy with cold hosing, or cool boots twice daily (don't use ice because it can burn);
➤ support bandaging (Tendon support bandaging p68) of both the affected limb and the one on the other side;
➤ medication to give pain relief and to reduce inflammation;
➤ in some cases surgical treatment, laser therapy or shock-wave therapy.
➤ A diagnosis of the exact injury can be made using diagnostic ultrasonography (Ultrasonography p112) and a convalescence plan appropriate to the injury (Exercise in convalescence p37) can be worked out, with regular diagnostic ultrasound examinations to check progress.

or putting a hoof down a rabbit hole. In order to assess the severity of such an injury it is important to determine the precise location of the injury, the structures it involves, and also the degree to which they are damaged. Without such information it is impossible to know what the likely outcome will be.

When a horse 'pulls a tendon' he is usually found to be acutely lame with swelling and heat in the region of these structures; even finger pressure applied to this area usually elicits a painful response.

AFTERCARE AND PROGNOSIS

Whether he regains his previous level of athletic performance, or starts a new job as a hack or field companion, a horse that has recovered from such an injury will always be at risk of recurrence of the injury. It is particularly important to ensure that such horses don't overstretch themselves, and if they are in work, to try to ensure that they are fit and their work level is kept fairly constant. Regular daily monitoring of the limbs for heat, pain, swelling and lameness is also advisable so that any problems can be picked up promptly, the horse immediately put on to box rest, and a vet called for further

- A subtle tendon injury may simply cause loss of definition of the structures of the limb, and can be hard to appreciate.

assessment. Prompt treatment always gives the best chance of a good outcome.

Buying a horse that has had a previous tendon injury always carries an element of increased risk, and diagnostic ultrasound to make a more detailed assessment of the original injury, and how well it has healed, can help decision-making in such cases.

What is diagnostic ultrasound?

Diagnostic ultrasound involves clipping the hair and then using an ultrasound probe on the skin over the affected area to image soft tissue structures. Good detail of tendon, ligament, muscle and fluid-filled structures can be derived, and abnormalities on the surface of bone can be seen, although ultrasound cannot penetrate bone and image its internal structure. Diagnostic ultrasound is particularly useful for imaging tendon, ligament and muscle, and organs such as the liver, spleen, kidneys and heart, and the surface of the lungs.

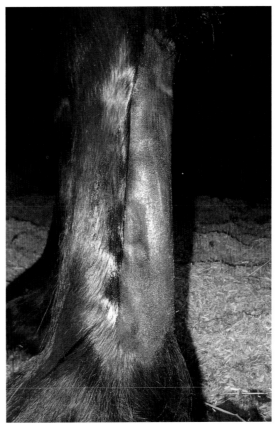

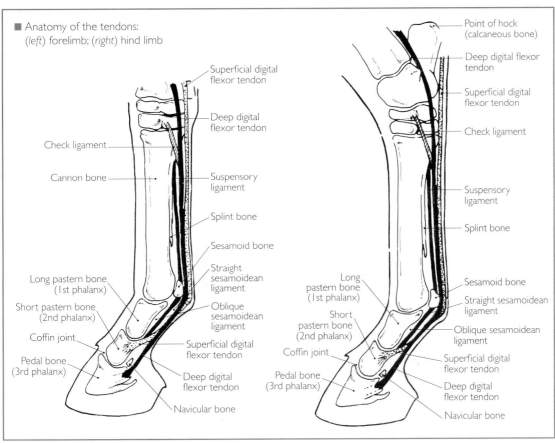

- Anatomy of the tendons:
  (*left*) forelimb; (*right*) hind limb

Forelimb:
- Superficial digital flexor tendon
- Deep digital flexor tendon
- Check ligament
- Cannon bone
- Suspensory ligament
- Splint bone
- Sesamoid bone
- Straight sesamoidean ligament
- Long pastern bone (1st phalanx)
- Short pastern bone (2nd phalanx)
- Oblique sesamoidean ligament
- Coffin joint
- Superficial digital flexor tendon
- Pedal bone (3rd phalanx)
- Deep digital flexor tendon
- Navicular bone

Hind limb:
- Point of hock (calcaneous bone)
- Deep digital flexor tendon
- Superficial digital flexor tendon
- Check ligament
- Suspensory ligament
- Splint bone
- Sesamoid bone
- Long pastern bone (1st phalanx)
- Straight sesamoidean ligament
- Short pastern bone (2nd phalanx)
- Oblique sesamoidean ligament
- Coffin joint
- Superficial digital flexor tendon
- Pedal bone (3rd phalanx)
- Deep digital flexor tendon
- Navicular bone

Is there anything I can do to prevent my young horse getting splints?

The splint bones are small bones that lie on either side of the canon bone, beneath the carpus. They articulate with the carpus (knee) or hock, and support part of the weight that is carried through the joint. They are held against the canon bone by strong ligaments called interosseous ligaments.

Excessive concussion, poor shoeing, obesity and poor conformation can, however, lead to abnormally high forces in this area, which causes inflammation in the region of the interosseous ligament. This can result in new bone being laid down around the splint bones (particularly the medial one, which bears the most weight), which in the long term may

What is scintigraphy?

Scintigraphy is another method that helps locate the site of an injury. It works by detecting increased blood flow or increased inflammation and healing, rather than pain *per se*, and is particularly useful for investigating horses that are not particularly lame, or that have head, neck or back problems. A non-toxic radioactive chemical is injected into the horse's bloodstream, and then the horse is scanned with a gamma camera that picks up emission of energy from the radioactive source. Images are formed on screen that show 'hot spots' of radiation energy in areas that are receiving a particularly high supply of blood or contain very rapidly dividing cells, indicating the site of inflammation or healing.

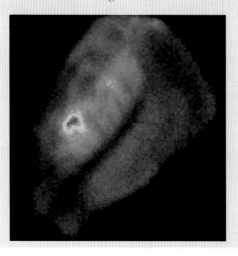

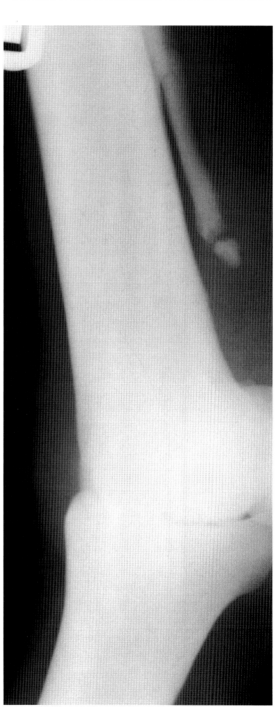

■ Fractures of the splint bones can occur. Most cases do well with rest, but some require surgery.

help to stabilize the area, but in the short term is associated with inflammation, heat, swelling, pain and lameness.

The typical horse that is affected is a young horse that suddenly develops painful swellings over the splint bones and can be lame. Suspensory ligament injuries may also occur (Tendon injuries p128), and in some cases similar symptoms may be seen following a knock to the splint bone (for example, due to brushing or a kick from another horse), which can even result in a fracture of the splint bone. Ultrasonography (Ultrasonography p112), radiography (Radiography p121) and scintigraphy (Scintigraphy p130) may therefore be required for a diagnosis to be made.

■ Even a large, prominent splint may cause no long term lameness, but veterinary advice should be sought.

TREATMENT

Treatment includes:

➤ box rest;

➤ support bandaging; and

➤ anti-inflammatory pain-relieving medicines can be used to allow splints to settle down, though this can take weeks to months.

➤ Occasionally surgery is indicated to reduce large splints, or to treat fractures or infected splint bones.

➤ Affected horses, and any horses that are young or susceptible, should avoid exercise on hard ground.

➤ Regular farriery is also helpful, and horses that brush will benefit from wearing brushing boots.

My horse has a lump near his hock. What could it be?

The hock has a very complex structure involving bones arranged in rows articulating in four different joints, and swellings in the area of the hock can relate to any of these bones or their associated ligaments and soft tissues. Although some conditions are not always associated with lameness in the early stages, and some may not cause lameness at all, always have any lumps and bumps checked promptly by a vet so that, where necessary, appropriate treatment can be instituted as quickly as possible, giving the best chance of recovery.

COMMON PROBLEMS
Bone spavin or osteoarthritis:
Bone spavin or osteoarthritis (Arthritis p135) of the hock leads to a gradual and slow onset of lameness which, in the early stages, is often only evident when the horse first moves off from rest. Eventually, however, it can lead to stiffness of the joints in the hock, pain, a shortened hind-limb stride, and dragging of the toes. Genetic factors may be involved in the development of this disease (it is particularly common in Icelandic Toelter horses), and it is also seen more commonly in horses that work at speed, but with sudden stops, such as Western horses. Clinical examination may allow diagnosis. Hock mobility is restricted, flexion tests (Flexion tests p120) usually increase the severity of lameness, and new bone may be deposited around the joint, including at the 'site of spavin', leading to a bony

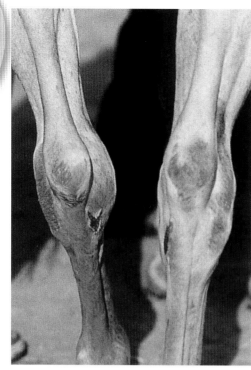

lump forming on the medial side (inside) of the limb at the bottom of the hock. Diagnosis may involve radiography (Radiography p121), scintigraphy (Scintigraphy p130) and joint blocks (Nerve and joint blocks p120).

Treatment includes low levels of exercise, also the systemic and intra-articular use of anti-inflammatory pain-relieving medicines, and, potentially, fusing of the affected joints, which can result in a more comfortable horse, even if movement remains partially restricted.

■ Bone spavin of the left hock (*left*).

■ Spavin (*below left*) involves arthritic change within the hock; note the loss of definition of the bones compared with a normal hock (*below right*).

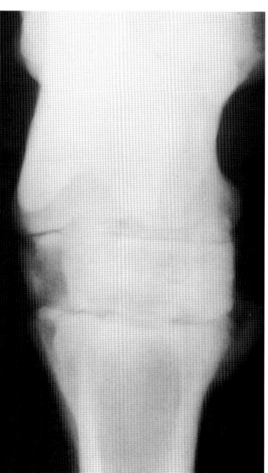

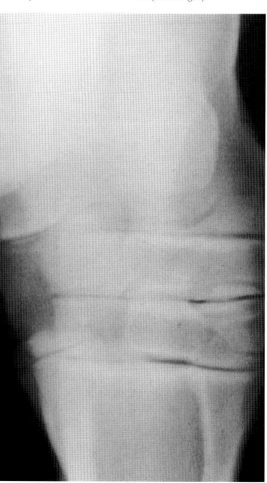

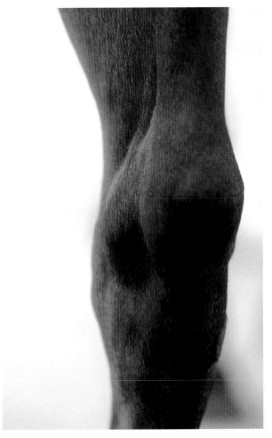

■ Bog spavin

(Arthrocentesis below), and treatment includes the use of anti-inflammatory medication and restricted levels of exercise.

Other problems in the region of the hock include:

Thoroughpin: soft swellings in the tarsal sheath that surrounds the hock joint just above the point of the hock on both sides of the limb.

Curb: a swelling situated on the back of the hock due to laxity of the palmar ligament that is responsible for holding the back of the hock in a straight line.

Bog spavin:

Bone spavin should not be confused with bog spavin or synovitis (inflammation) of the hock, which leads to soft, fluctuant swelling of the joint. Predisposing factors include the development of arthritic change in the joint (Arthritis p135) and OCD (OCD p134), as well as hocks that are too straight, or have a sickle- or cow-hocked conformation. Affected horses are typically lame with a reduced forward phase to the hind-limb stride and poor hock flexion. Examination to elucidate the underlying cause includes radiography (Radiography p121) and also arthrocentesis

What is arthrocentesis?

This involves the sampling of joint fluid in sterile conditions (to avoid causing joint infection (Joint infection p136)) for microscopic examination. This allows the identification of increased inflammatory proteins (which can indicate joint inflammation and arthritis) as well as bacteria and white blood cells (which can indicate infection).

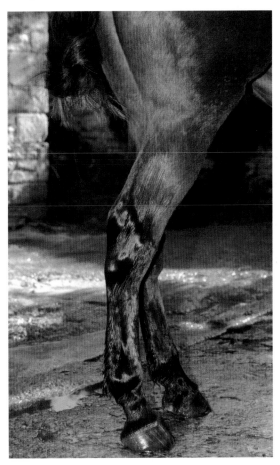

■ Curb

Damage to the superficial digital flexor tendon as it passes over the point of the hock: this can result in an abnormal contour in the area, and so also abnormal gait.

Any such swellings should be evaluated promptly by a vet so that a diagnosis can be made and appropriate treatment instituted.

What is OCD? Can it be avoided, and how is it treated?

OCD or OC (osteochondrosis) is a developmental bone disease generally seen in strong foals that grow quickly on an over-rich diet with mineral imbalances (Feeding p23). Over-exercise on growing limbs is another factor in the development of this disease. Genetics are also involved.

The disease is characterized by the development of abnormal, weak cartilage that is easily damaged, leading to fragmentation of the articular surfaces of bone within the joints. Cysts, flaps of damaged cartilage and roughened cartilage can all occur, leading to inflammation, poor mobility and pain. Typical symptoms include joint swelling, pain and lameness, with the stifles, hocks, elbows, shoulders, carpus and fetlocks being most commonly affected. Affected foals and yearlings may lie down a lot, and may also find it hard to keep up with their peers, even if they do not show any signs of obvious lameness.

Ultrasonography (p112), as well as radiography (p121), and arthrocentesis (p133) can all aid a vet in his/her diagnosis.

■ A hock affected by OCD. OCD has caused loss of cartilage, which has led to bone fragmentation within the joint, resulting in joint swelling and lameness.

TREATMENT

Treatment is based on:

➤ restricted exercise and food;

➤ the use of anti-inflammatory medicines (Medication p72); and,

➤ in some cases, arthroscopy (Arthroscopy, *see* below) to remove damaged tissue from the affected joints.

What is arthroscopy?

Arthroscopy involves the introduction of a small 'scope', like an endoscope, into a joint through a tiny surgical hole in the skin, in order to inspect and evaluate the cartilage, bone and ligamentar structures within the joint. Small instruments may then be introduced through another minute hole, and used to remove damaged tissue where this is necessary. This process is normally carried out under general anaesthesia, and also involves flushing the joint with large volumes of fluids and antibiotics to remove debris and prevent infection.

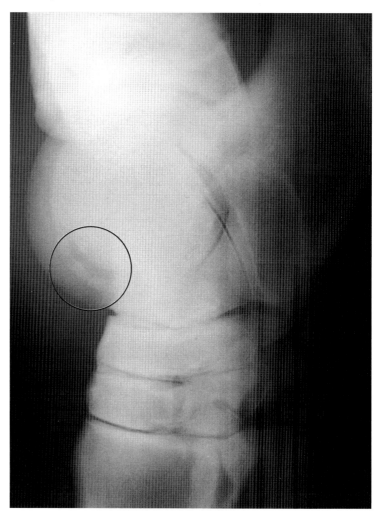

How much of a problem is arthritis in horses?

As in any species, age-related wear and tear and joint injuries result in damage within the joints, which causes varying degrees of osteoarthritis or degenerative joint disease. Ligament damage, cartilage damage and fractures involving the joints all contribute to a roughened joint surface and a reduction in the viscosity of joint fluid, which reduces its lubricating properties. New bone is then laid down in and around the joints as part of a vicious circle that leads to further roughening of the joint surfaces and loss of joint mobility. The consequence is the development of stiffness and joint pain. Some horses develop arthritic change in single joints after an injury, whilst others develop it in multiple joints due to genetic factors, overwork, obesity or old age.

Clinical examination (Examination pp57–8) and flexion tests (Flexion tests p120) can assist diagnosis, nerve and joint blocks (Nerve and joint blocks p120) can allow localization of the sources of most significant pain, and radiography (Radiography p121) is useful for allowing assessment of affected joints.

TREATMENT

➤ In rare cases surgical treatment – for example, arthroscopy (Arthroscopy p134) – may be helpful, but most affected horses are treated medically.

➤ Some medications and nutraceuticals are used that aim to improve cartilage repair and joint fluid viscosity, whilst other medicines are used to reduce inflammation and provide pain relief.

➤ Medicines may be used systemically where multiple joints are involved, or they may be delivered directly into the affected joint if a single joint is affected. But despite treatment, many old horses in time gradually become stiffer, and their level of performance and agility inevitably reduces.

➤ Complementary therapies including acupuncture (Acupuncture p13) may be useful in some cases.

■ Ringbone or arthritic change in the pastern area can cause joint pain and stiffness.

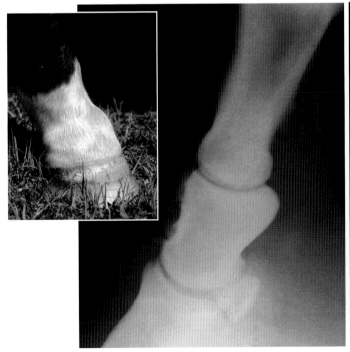

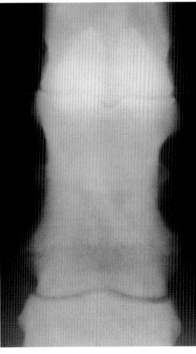

What causes joint infections? How are they treated?

One of the most significant risks with wounds in the vicinity of joints and tendon sheaths (both known as synovial structures because they are bathed in synovial fluid) is that of infection of these structures. The problem is that synovial infections can be hard (and expensive), if not impossible, to treat in the horse, and the result of infection of joints or tendons can be a chronically infected structure that remains weak and painful and can't heal.

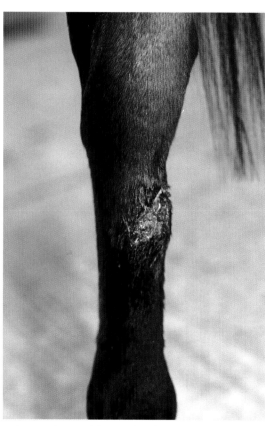

■ A wound near a joint needs to be taken very seriously as the site may become infected with dire results.

TREATMENT

Treatment involves:

➤ Flushing of the affected structure with large volumes of fluids and antibiotics. This usually has to be done under general anaesthetic, and is therefore quite costly.

➤ Long courses of antibiotics also need to be used, and the period of convalescence can be extensive.

➤ Where such wounds (Wounds pp64, 85) are identified or suspected, it is essential that the horse has early veterinary attention and prompt referral to a hospital facility in order to ensure the best chance of recovery.

➤ Arthrocentesis can allow identification of whether bacterial contamination or infection is present, and further tests including radiography and ultrasonography may also be necessary. Whilst such measures may seem excessive with apparently minor wounds, it is always better to be over-cautious in such situations.

Symptoms include swelling and severe pain, as well as high temperature and lack of appetite. In some cases, euthanasia becomes the only option. However, those cases that involve injury to synovial structures may respond well to treatment as long as that treatment is prompt (preferably within four hours of the injury), and intensive.

Other causes of joint infections include spread of infection through the bloodstream, and inadvertent introduction of bacteria when joint blocks (Nerve and joint blocks p120), arthrocentesis (Arthrocentesis p133) or intra-articular medication (Medication p72) is being carried out.

Diagnosis includes arthrocentesis (Arthrocentesis p133), radiography (Radiography p121), and finally scintigraphy (Scintigraphy p130).

Do all fractures necessitate euthanasia?

■ Following this crashing fall both horse and rider walked away, but fractures caused by major trauma can be fatal.

Although some fractures can be fixed, the sheer bodyweight of the horse, combined with his behavioural and physical need to remain standing rather than to submit to being nursed lying down, together mean that most spine and many limb fractures are catastrophic and necessitate euthanasia of the affected horse. Fatal fractures include most of those that affect the longbones in the limbs, often causing an obviously disrupted 'swinging' leg, or a horse that is unable to rise (Recumbency p60). These sorts of injuries may occur out in the field, or following accidents associated with cars, bolting on to rough terrain, or kicks.

TREATMENT

➤ Fractures that can be treated include some stress fractures that occur in racehorses, and various partial or uni-cortical fractures (ones that only involve one side of the bone) that do not initially result in complete collapse of the affected bone.

➤ Since it can be hard to make an assessment as to the cause of the problem, horses with suspected fractures should receive immediate veterinary attention.

➤ Where possible, pain-relieving medications and sedatives can then be used to allow support bandaging or splinting (Splinting p68) of the affected limb in order to prevent further injury while the horse is transported to a hospital for further assessment.

➤ Those horses whose pain is uncontrollable or that have obviously catastrophic fractures should be immediately euthanased on humane grounds.

My horse is 'cold-backed': have you any suggestions as to what I can do?

Horses that resent being saddled or girthed up, bearing a rider, or even, in some cases, having their back stroked and groomed, may have back pain, or behavioural problems that are sometimes related to previous back pain. Whatever the cause of this kind of behaviour, however, it is important to ensure that there are no underlying problems:

➤ The most usual cause of back pain is poor saddle fit, so one of the first steps is to contact a master saddler (Tack p22) and have the saddle fit and flocking checked, even if it wasn't long since the saddler last came (even small amounts of weight loss or gain, or changes in musculature, can result in the saddle no longer fitting).
➤ Ensure that the horse's riders are not causing a problem by poor riding or by being too heavy for the horse.
➤ A veterinary check is also advisable, and this can allow a thorough evaluation of the back and identification of any painful areas.
➤ It is also important to have the horse checked for lameness, as subtle lamenesses sometimes cause back pain due to changes in the horse's mobility,

rather than obvious limping. Further investigation may be necessary, and to this end ultrasonography (Ultrasonography p112) can allow evaluation of the muscles of the back and the contours of the spine and pelvis. Radiography (Radiography p121) can allow assessment of the spine, and can allow identification of 'kissing spines' that are too close together and cause pain by impinging one upon another. Scintigraphy (Scintigraphy p130) is often useful, and thermography (Thermography p126) may also be used.

➤ Initial treatment often includes the use of anti-inflammatory pain-relieving medicines (Medicines p72), and these can be employed for a two-week 'pain trial' to try and evaluate whether the horse's symptoms are genuinely associated with pain, or whether there is a behavioural problem.
➤ Rest may be helpful, but in many cases it is more useful to initiate a controlled exercise regime to keep the horse mobile without allowing matters to worsen. Complementary therapies such as physiotherapy (Physiotherapy p13), chiropracty (Chiropracty p13) and acupuncture (Acupuncture p13) are also often useful.

■ A thorough examination of the back may allow identification of the cause of a 'cold back'.

My endurance horse ties up: what can I do?

Also known as azoturia, setfast and exertional rhabdomyolysis, tying up is a condition that involves an excessive response to exercise, with muscle damage and consequent back and hind-limb muscle pain, cramping and, potentially, collapse. Abnormal urination may also be seen, with urine that is darkened because it contains broken-down muscle proteins; other symptoms include distress, breathing difficulties and muscle tremors. Kidney disease can also develop, as the high levels of muscle proteins and enzymes in the blood can cause kidney failure.

The condition is most usual in endurance horses and quarter horses, and is generally seen in horses that exercise at levels beyond their training, or that return to work too quickly after a period of rest. It can also be seen in horses that have recently recovered from viral infections. In addition, some horses appear to be predisposed to this condition, and despite careful training and management, suffer repeatedly. Although diagnosis of the condition is usually based on the typical clinical signs, blood tests to check for enzymes indicating muscle damage can also be helpful, and tests for certain nutrient levels (Feeding p24) may also be appropriate.

TREATMENT

Emergency treatment includes:

➤ fluid therapy (these horses generally need to go on a drip);

➤ muscle relaxants; and

➤ pain-killers.

Avoidance incorporates:

➤ suitable training regimes that include a sufficient warm-up and cool-down time (Exercise p37).

➤ Appropriate nutrition with low carbohydrate and higher fibre and fat levels is advisable, and

➤ the use of supplementary nutrients and electrolytes (Feeding pp24–26) may also be necessary.

Fillies that tie up when in season may benefit from the medical suppression of oestrus (Medication p72), and all horses benefit from a consistent regime of feeding and exercise with the minimum of changes.

■ It is best to avoid stabling horses that are prone to tie up.

My horse keeps going wobbly: what could cause this?

COMMON DISEASES

Nerve-related conditions in the horse are not particularly common, but are usually devastating when they do occur because of the safety implications of weakness or collapse: whether under saddle, in harness, or even being led, a weak and wobbly horse is potentially very dangerous.

Problems that cause 'wobbliness' can generally be divided into those that are associated with the brain not working properly, and those that result from problems in the body – although some problems may affect both. Brain disorders may be associated with neurological symptoms ranging from weakness, loss of balance, circling and collapse, to blindness, behavioural changes, fitting (which can also be manifested as sudden sleeping or 'narcolepsy') and

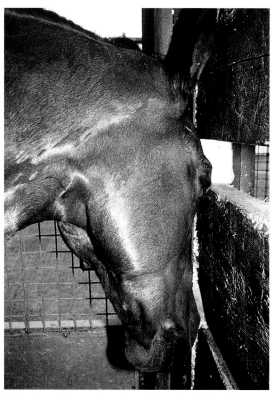

■ Head pressing can be a sign of neurological problems.

TREATMENT

Because neurological diseases can be so unpredictable and so dangerous it is important to seek prompt veterinary attention.

➤ In addition, it is helpful to videotape any abnormal behaviour, as symptoms can be intermittent and may not be apparent when the vet is present.

➤ A vet's full neurological examination can include testing of cranial nerves (involved in sight, hearing, balance, smell and eating), brain, body and limb reflexes and mobility.

➤ In addition, it may be advisable to perform blood tests and further examinations that may include radiography (Radiography p121), head MRI (MRI p125), and scintigraphy (Scintigraphy p130).

However, it should be borne in mind that most neurological diseases are difficult, if not impossible to treat, and retirement or euthanasia are the likely outcomes.

head pressing (when horses press their heads against the wall). Peripheral nervous problems tend to be more associated with weakness of the limbs, paralysis, muscle wastage and poor co-ordination. Lameness, toe dragging and stumbling may also be seen, and pain can be a factor.

Other potential problems include difficulty swallowing (Choke p104), laryngeal paralysis (Laryngeal disease p100), and incontinence or bladder paralysis. Such symptoms can relate to injuries, tumours, inflammatory disease, infections (such as herpes virus), narrowing of the spinal canal (wobbler disease), or underlying disorders such as parasitic worm migration (Worming p17) or liver disease (Liver disease p109). Also, in the USA, equine protozoal myeloencephalitis, encephalomyelitis virus and rabies are always on the list of possibilities.

My mare seems very lethargic. Could she be anaemic?

The causes of lethargy range from heart disease (Heart disease p93), respiratory disease (Respiratory disease p96), musculoskeletal problems (Lameness p119), liver and kidney disorders (Liver disease p109, Urinary disease p111) and neurological problems (Neurological disease p140), to blood diseases, poor nutrition (Feeding p23) and worms (Worms p17). Whilst anaemia can be associated with lethargy, it is rarely a major primary problem in horses unless they have recently suffered a major haemorrhage (Blood loss p62). However, any signs of abnormal behaviour or lethargy should be investigated promptly by a vet, and one of the first steps of such an investigation would be to perform blood tests that would identify anaemia and a range of other potential causes of non-specific symptoms such as lethargy.

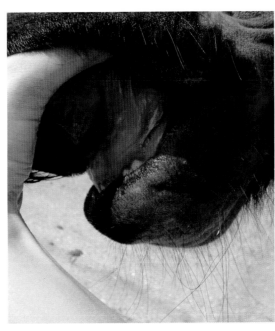

■ The gum colour can be checked to identify any obvious signs of anaemia or abnormal circulation.

My previous horse died of a blood cancer: how common is this?

Various types of cancer can affect the horse, as other species, and whilst some cause the growth of solid masses that can affect the skin (Skin masses p83), internal organs, and limbs and spine (Neurological disease p140) causing a variety of symptoms, others may affect the bone marrow or lymph systems, resulting in cancerous cells circulating in the blood. These types of cancer are thankfully rare, but occur unpredictably with no identified trigger factors that are avoidable.

Symptoms of blood disorders – and disorders can be due to tumours, liver disease or immune deficiency – include increased susceptibility to infections, anaemia, circulatory problems, swellings, and clotting disorders that cause abnormal bleeding and bruising. Any such symptoms should be investigated promptly by a vet.

What causes a fat leg and what will make it go down?

Almost anything that causes a limb to swell can result in lymphoedema (poor lymph drainage of the affected area), which causes persistent limb swelling. Injuries (Wounds pp64, 85) and infections such as cellulitis (infection and inflammation of the tissues under the skin) are commonly involved, but heart disease (Heart disease p93) and allergic (Allergies p81) or toxic reactions (such as to snake bites) can also cause severe limb swelling and oedema.

TREATMENT

In the early stages options include:

➤ gentle exercise to help disperse swellings (unless this is contra-indicated for any reason);

➤ cold hosing;

➤ support bandaging (Support bandaging p68) and

➤ massaging of affected limbs.

Anti-inflammatory medication may also be useful, and in some cases corticosteroids are used. However, despite treatment, the affected limb may stay persistently swollen, or consistently swell after rest, and this swelling can cause stiffness and may affect mobility.

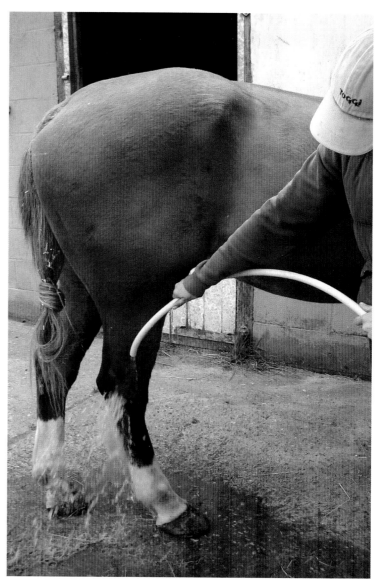

■ Cold hosing can help reduce limb swelling.

Someone told me my pony might have Cushing's: what is this?

Cushing's disease is a hormonal disease that, in the horse or pony, relates to swelling of the pituitary gland at the base of the brain, and overactivity of this gland. The result is that the adrenal gland is over-stimulated and produces an excessive amount of the natural steroids that are needed at low levels for normal body function. Like any hormonal disease, high steroid levels in cushingoid horses (or more often old ponies) cause a wide range of symptoms, from immune suppression to muscle wastage, weight loss (Weight loss p107), retention of the winter coat, increased drinking and laminitis (Laminitis p122). Swelling of the fat pads above the eyes is also commonly seen. In many cases retention of the winter coat is the first symptom seen, whilst in others, repeated bouts of laminitis that respond poorly to treatment are the presenting complaint.

TREATMENT

➤ Whatever the symptoms, the disease can be confirmed using blood tests, and may be treated with medicines that suppress steroid production. Such medication can be expensive though, and since most of the animals that suffer from this condition are ancient ponies that are already retired, specific treatment is not always carried out. Instead supportive treatment and careful management (Laminitis p122) may be used to minimize any effects on the patient's quality of life.

■ Cushing's syndrome is not uncommon in elderly ponies. It causes weight loss, retention of the winter coat, and an increased tendency to develop laminitis.

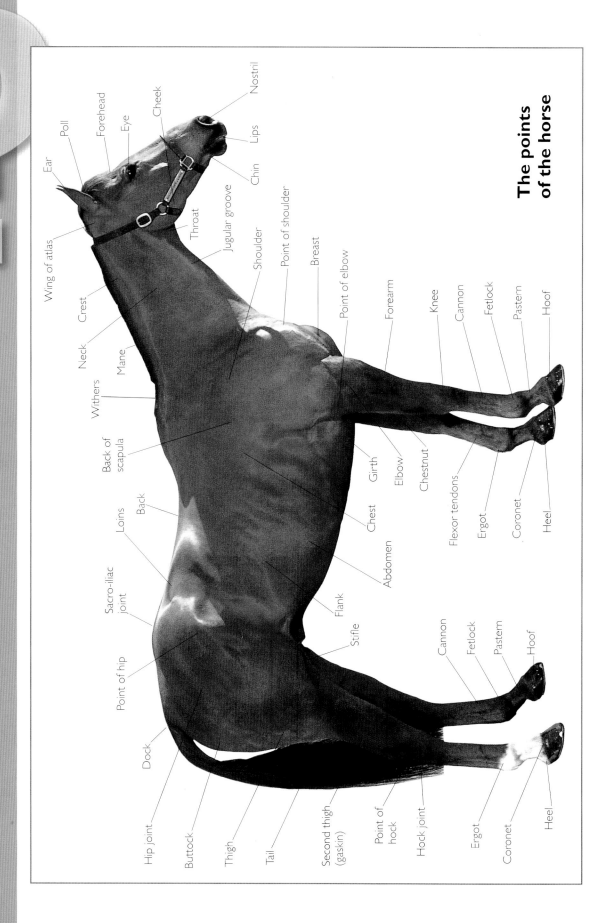

The points of the horse

Ear
Poll
Forehead
Eye
Cheek
Nostril
Lips
Chin
Throat
Jugular groove
Shoulder
Point of shoulder
Breast
Point of elbow
Forearm
Knee
Cannon
Fetlock
Pastern
Hoof
Wing of atlas
Crest
Neck
Mane
Withers
Back of scapula
Back
Loins
Sacro-iliac joint
Point of hip
Dock
Hip joint
Buttock
Thigh
Tail
Second thigh (gaskin)
Point of hock
Hock joint
Ergot
Coronet
Heel
Cannon
Fetlock
Pastern
Hoof
Stifle
Flank
Abdomen
Chest
Girth
Elbow
Chestnut
Flexor tendons
Ergot
Coronet
Heel

The horse's skeleton

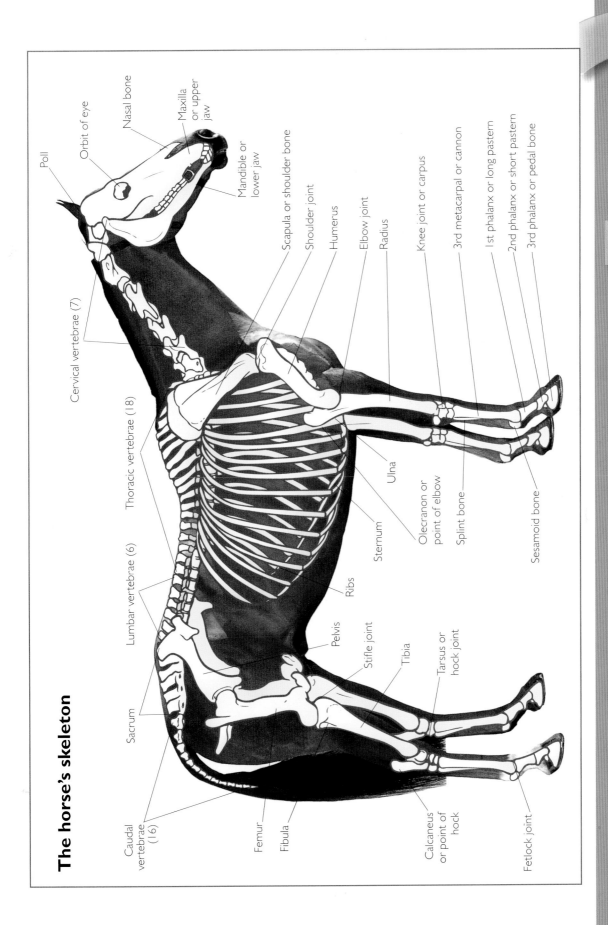

Poll
Orbit of eye
Nasal bone
Maxilla or upper jaw
Mandible or lower jaw
Scapula or shoulder bone
Shoulder joint
Humerus
Elbow joint
Radius
Knee joint or carpus
3rd metacarpal or cannon
1st phalanx or long pastern
2nd phalanx or short pastern
3rd phalanx or pedal bone

Cervical vertebrae (7)
Thoracic vertebrae (18)
Lumbar vertebrae (6)
Sacrum
Caudal vertebrae (16)

Femur
Fibula
Pelvis
Stifle joint
Tibia
Tarsus or hock joint

Calcaneus or point of hock
Fetlock joint

Ulna
Olecranon or point of elbow
Splint bone
Sternum
Ribs
Sesamoid bone

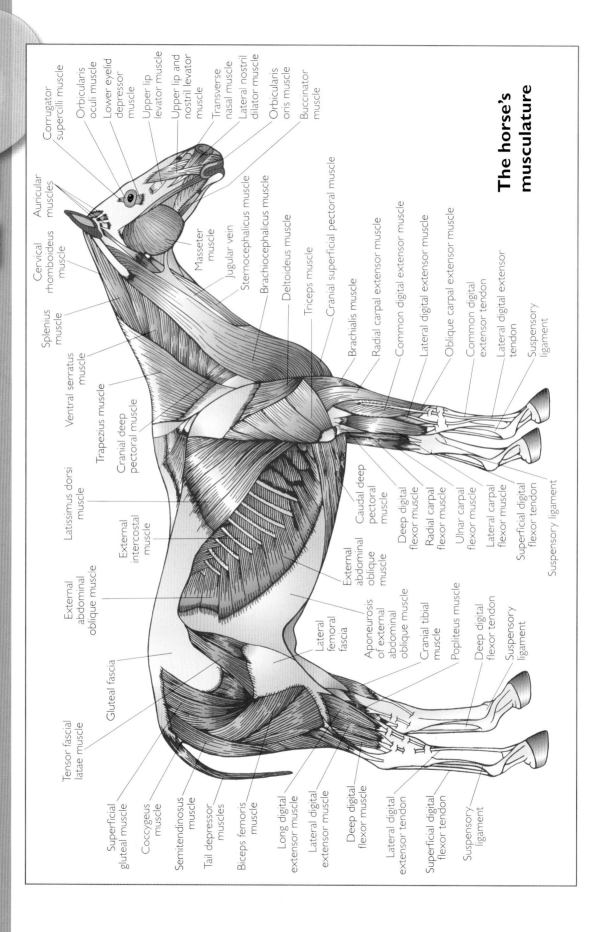

The horse's musculature

Corrugator supercilii muscle
Orbicularis oculi muscle
Lower eyelid depressor muscle
Upper lip levator muscle
Upper lip and nostril levator muscle
Transverse nasal muscle
Lateral nostril dilator muscle
Orbicularis oris muscle
Buccinator muscle

Auricular muscles
Cervical rhomboideus muscle
Masseter muscle
Jugular vein
Sternocephalicus muscle
Brachiocephalicus muscle
Deltoideus muscle
Cranial superficial pectoral muscle

Splenius muscle
Triceps muscle
Brachialis muscle
Radial carpal extensor muscle
Common digital extensor muscle
Lateral digital extensor muscle
Oblique carpal extensor muscle
Common digital extensor tendon
Lateral digital extensor tendon
Suspensory ligament

Ventral serratus muscle
Trapezius muscle
Cranial deep pectoral muscle

Tensor fascial latae muscle
Gluteal fascia

Latissimus dorsi muscle

External abdominal oblique muscle

External intercostal muscle

Caudal deep pectoral muscle
Deep digital flexor muscle
Radial carpal flexor muscle
Ulnar carpal flexor muscle
Lateral carpal flexor muscle
Superficial digital flexor tendon
Suspensory ligament

External abdominal oblique muscle

Lateral femoral fascia
Aponeurosis of external abdominal oblique muscle
Cranial tibial muscle
Popliteus muscle
Deep digital flexor tendon
Suspensory ligament

Superficial gluteal muscle
Coccygeus muscle
Semitendinosus muscle
Tail depressor muscles
Biceps femoris muscle
Long digital extensor muscle
Lateral digital extensor muscle
Deep digital flexor muscle
Lateral digital extensor tendon
Superficial digital flexor tendon
Suspensory ligament

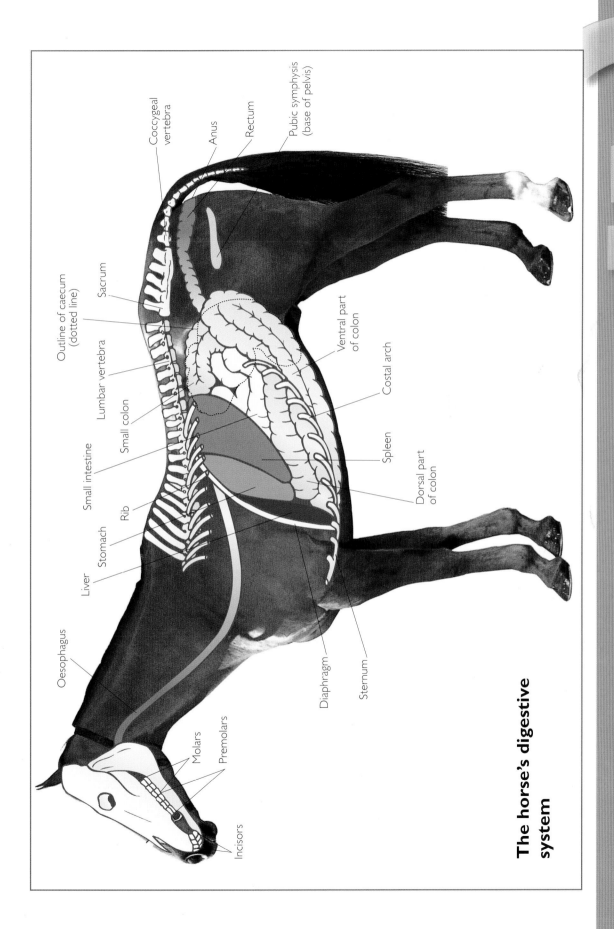

Oesophagus

Molars

Premolars

Incisors

Liver

Stomach

Rib

Small intestine

Small colon

Lumbar vertebra

Outline of caecum
(dotted line)

Sacrum

Coccygeal
vertebra

Anus

Rectum

Pubic symphysis
(base of pelvis)

Ventral part
of colon

Costal arch

Spleen

Dorsal part
of colon

Diaphragm

Sternum

**The horse's digestive
system**

Conclusion

Having a horse is, for many of us, one of the most rewarding experiences in our lives. To help our horses to be healthy and happy, we need to ensure that they are well looked after. They need to be provided with a safe and comfortable environment, appropriate preventative healthcare, a satisfactory diet and a suitable level of exercise. And when, as sometimes happens, things go wrong, it is important to be able to make a rapid assessment of the severity of any problem and to institute appropriate first aid pending the attendance of a veterinary surgeon. In order to give the best health care to horses it is important to use professionals that are trusted and whose advice owners are happy to follow.

The aim of this book is to furnish owners with the information they need to keep their horses well, and to deal appropriately with any problems that occur in order to give horses the best chance of a speedy recovery.

Nature is always a great healer. Our responsibility is to do all that we can to help our horses to stay healthy, and when treatable problems occur, to provide them with the best environment for the natural processes of healing so that a prompt recovery can follow.

Glossary

abortion miscarriage

adsorbent substance that can accumulate other substances eg toxins/ poisons to reduce their absorption in the body

allergen substance that causes an allergic reaction

anaemia reduction in red blood cells

anorexia reduced appetite

anti-inflammatory medicine that reduces inflammation

anti-oxidant substance that reduces cell damage

antibiotic medicine that treats bacterial infection

arrythmia abnormal heart rhythm

arytenoids structures in the larynx

atrophy wastage

Aubiose bedding material

bacteria small organism. Some can cause infection/ disease, others are needed in the body for normal digestion and function

benzimidazole type of wormer

bit-seating way of tooth-rasping that aids positioning of, and response to, the bit

biopsy sample of tissue

bot type of fly that has larval stage within the horse

brushing (feet) close movement of limbs that can cause self-injury

cardiovascular of the heart and circulation

chemotherapy medicine used to treat tumours

Chifney type of bit that aids control of horse when leading

chorioptes type of skin mite

colic abdominal pain

colostrum first milk that contains immune products

compounded/ concentrate feed commercial feed containing a mixture of ingredients, often high in starch (see short feed)

conformation build/ physical attributes

crib-biting vice involving biting on to fences and suchlike

cryotherapy use of freezing to treat disease

cyathostomes type of roundworm

dermatitis skin disease

dishing (feet) 'flicking out' movement of lower limbs that can predispose to injury

dorsal displacement of the soft palate abnormal movement of the structures near the larynx that causes gulping and severe loss of performance

encysted formed into a cyst (for instance, worms in the body)

endometritis womb infection

endotoxaemia spread of infection and toxins into the blood

epiglottic entrapment abnormal movement of the structures near the larynx that causes a serious loss of performance

epiglottis structure next to the larynx that normally prevents inhalation of food

euthanasia killing for humane reasons

exudates oozed fluid (eg from wound)

facial/ maxillary artery blood vessels in the face where a pulse can be felt

feed balancers food additive that contains necessary nutrients

fibre nutrient in forage needed for digestion

foetus unborn foal

forage grass/ pasture/ hay-based food

fructan type of sugar found at varying quantities in grass

hemiplegia paralysis on one side

hypertrophy over-development

immunotherapy medicine that has an effect on the immune system

impaction gut blockage

infertile unable to reproduce

intestinal absorption tests tests to check how well the guts can absorb foods and function

intestines guts

laparoscopy insertion of a small camera into the abdomen to look at the organs

laparotomy surgical opening of the abdomen

laser therapy use of laser to treat disease

local small affected area

macrocyclic lactone type of wormer

murmur abnormal heart sound

oedema swelling under the skin that relates to fluid retention

oesophagus gullet that takes food from mouth to stomach

palpation feeling affected areas

peritoneum lining of the abdomen

photoactive substance that reacts to light

photosensitization area that is made more sensitive by light

plaiting (feet) crossing of lower limbs

during motion that can predispose to injuries

probiotic substance that promotes development of bacteria necessary for health

prolapse slipping out of place (eg of an organ)

pruritis itchiness

pulmonary of the lungs

radiotherapy use of radioactivity to treat disease (eg tumours)

rectum lower bowel

redworm type of roundworm

resistance development of organism so that it no longer responds to treatment

roundworm type of worm that is round in cross-section

short feed grain/cereal-based feed (see concentrate/ compounded feed) that is usually high in starch

soft palate tissue between throat and passages of the nose

solar injury injury to the sole of the foot

stale urinate/ pass water

sterile 1) infertility 2) sufficient cleanliness that bacteria are eliminated

strongyles roundworms

sub-solar infection infection under the sole of the foot

subfertile less fertile than normal (ie difficult to breed from)

systemic something that spreads through the whole body (eg medication or infection)

tapeworm type of worm that has a flat, tape-like structure

tetrahydropyrimidine type of wormer

tooth eruption when the growing tooth appears through the gum

topical treatment applied to skin surface

toxin poison (can be external eg chemical or plant, or released by bacteria internally)

turbid thick, lumpy

urticaria hives, swellings on the skin

virus tiny particle that can cause infection/ disease

weaving vice involving swaying from side to side that puts undue strain on the front legs

wind-sucking vice involving drawing in air and swallowing it, that can predispose to colic

worm larvae immature form of worms

Useful contacts and further reading

American Association of Equine Practitioners (AAEP) www.aaep.org 859 223 0147

American Holistic Veterinary Medical Association (AHVMA) www.ahvma.org 410 569 0795

American Veterinary Chiropractic Association (AVCA) www.animalciropractic.org 918 784 2231

American Farriers Association www.americanfarriers.org

American Society for the Prevention of Cruelty to Animals (ASPCA) www.aspca.org 212 876 7700

American Veterinary Medical Association (AVMA) www.avma.org 847 925 8070

Association of British Veterinary Acupuncturists (ABVA) abva.co.uk

Association of British Riding Schools (ABRS) www.abrs.org

Association of Chartered Physiotherapists specialising in Animal Therapy (ACPAT) www.acpat.org.uk

British Association of Equine Dental Technicians (BAEDT) www.equinedentistry.org.uk

British Association of Homoeopathic Veterinary Surgeons (BAHVS) www.bahvs.com

British Equine Veterinary Association (BEVA) www.beva.org.uk 01223 836970

British Veterinary Association (BVA) www.bva.co.uk 0207 636 6541

British Horse Society (BHS) www.bhs.org.uk 08701 202244

Farriers Registration Council www.farrier-reg.gov.uk 01733 319911

Fédération Equestrian Internationale (FEI) www.horsesport.org

Horserace Betting Levy Board (HBLB) www.hblb.org.uk

International Veterinary Acupuncture Society (IVAS) www.ivas.org 970 266 0666

International League for the Protection of Horses (ILPH) www.ilph.org 01953 498682

Jockey Club www.thejockeyclub.co.uk (UK) www.jockeyclub.com (USA)

Master Saddlers Association www.mastersaddlers.com

McTimoney Chiropractic Association (MCA) www.mctimoney-chiropractic.org

Royal College of Veterinary Surgeons (RCVS) www.rcvs.org.uk 020 7222 2001

Royal Society for the Prevention of Cruelty to Animals (RSPCA) www.rspca.org.uk

Society of Master Saddlers www.mastersaddlers.co.uk

UK Horsewatch www.ukhorsewatch.org.uk

World Wide Association of Equine Dentists www.wwaed.org

FURTHER READING

Baker, Gordon and Easley, Jack *Equine Dentistry* W.B. Saunders, 2000 (ISBN 0-7020-2392-2).

Baxter, Roberta *Horse Injuries, their Prevention and Treatment* The Crowood Press, 1999 (ISBN 1-86126-260-4).

Britton, Vanessa *The Horse Owner's Problem Solver* David and Charles, 2003 (ISBN 0-7153-1317-7).

Britton, Vanessa *The Horse Rider's Problem Solver* David and Charles, 1997 (ISBN 0-7153-0613-8).

Index